PUBLISH YOUR KNOWLEDGE

THE COMPLETE GUIDE TO CROWDFUNDING A NONFICTION BOOK ON KICKSTARTER AND SELF-PUBLISHING THROUGH AMAZON

VILIUS STANISLOVAITIS

DOWNLOAD FREE BONUS

NONFICTION WRITING TIPS

Just to say thanks for reading my book,
I would like to give you this Free Bonus! Enjoy!
Go to: https://bit.ly/PublishYourKnowledge

CONTENTS

INTRODUCTION

> *"If there's a book that you want to read, but it hasn't been written yet, then you must write it."*
> —*Toni Morrison*

Writing a book is one of the best ways to share your expertise and get your message out into the world. The habit of writing helps you reflect and learn. You will expand your knowledge, gain greater expertise, develop new skills, and get a deeper understanding of your subject. This book is meant for aspiring writers who want to turn their expertise into a book, and those who wish to improve their entrepreneurial mindset along with their writing and self-publishing skills.

I know that many first-time authors struggle with the sales of their first book so I decided to share my story for those who:

- have an outside job or a small business and have always dreamed of writing a book one day;

- are considering writing their first nonfiction book (if you want to write a novel, this book might not be a good fit for you);

- don't know how to market and sell their first book;

- have written and self-published one or a few books, but sales didn't go that well.

This book is for those who write nonfiction. However, nonfiction is a very broad category that includes history, philosophy, journalism, memoirs, travel guides, academic texts, self-help, etc. To be more specific, the subcategory of my books is *guides* and *how-to manuals*. If you write or plan to write in a similar subcategory, you will get the most value from this book as my examples will be the most relevant to you. If your subcategory is another one, my examples may not be ideal for you, but the principles of writing, marketing, and selling any other nonfiction genres are very similar.

I'll be transparent with you. I can teach only what I have achieved myself. Here's a quick summary of what I did and what the results were:

- I created a ten-page guide *How to Start a VoIP Business* in two weeks.

- I uploaded it to the website as a freebie (lead magnet).

- Downloads started organically and I received positive feedback from readers.

- There was no book on this topic, so I decided to write a complete book.

- It took me five years to finish the manuscript—yes, a bit slow.

- I wasn't sure if there would be a demand for my book (it was very niche), so I decided to launch a Kickstarter campaign to validate my idea. For those who don't know, Kickstarter is a global crowdfunding platform that helps bring creative projects to life.

- Preparation for the Kickstarter campaign took two months.

- The Kickstarter campaign was successful. I raised $8,379 from 200 backers within 35 days.

- I did direct marketing to an additional list of potential readers not exposed to the Kickstarter campaign, and generated $1,837 through direct sales to this list.

- I self-published the book and shipped it to my Kickstarter backers and those who pre-ordered the book,

- I uploaded the book to Amazon, IngramSpark, and Smashwords. To date, it has generated another $5,513 in passive income (87% of this came from Amazon).

To date, I have made over $15,000 income from my first book and my profit was around $10,000. The real value was not in money, but in the experience I received. I became an expert in my industry, learned how to write books faster and wrote my second book in less than a year, came to understand that it is possible to create passive income by writing content, continued building my author platform and have created and maintained an automated process that converts prospects into paying customers. Now I have set a long-term goal of covering my living expenses from passive income by creating content (whether it's in written or another form) and sharing my experience with others.

Is this something you are seeking too?

If so, grab a cup of coffee and read how you can get started with your first book. I'll share what I've learned during my path and how you can adapt it to your case. The book is quite straightforward. You can read it quickly and take immediate action.

GET IN THE RIGHT MINDSET BEFORE YOU START

What is your number one goal in writing your book? Let yourself think about it for a while. Don't hurry. When you are fully satisfied with the answer, write it down on a piece of paper.

When I was writing my first book, my main goal was to make the book available on Amazon. That's all. Having my book published on the largest online book retailer in the world sounded like a solid lifetime achievement.

That doesn't mean I wasn't ambitious. Deep inside, I expected that my target audience would enjoy reading it, and that the book would be profitable. But I think that setting the right expectations—not too high, not too low—is much better than overestimating your possibilities. Even though I set low expectations, I managed to make $10,000 income from my first book before I even published it.

Remember, my goal wasn't to make money from the book. Income from book sales is a natural result that shows that readers see value in what the author shares and agree to exchange their money to get this value. My goal was to write a good how-to book and publish it on Amazon, but the initial reason *why* I decided to take on this challenge was something else.

Finding Your "Why"

There are many people that have "write a book at some point in my life" in their bucket list. However, just a few percent of those who dream of becoming an author actually write and publish their book because it is a monumental challenge for most people. Finding your "why" can get you in the right mindset before you start working on your book.

My *why* was to enrich my knowledge and share it with others. Without the context of the story, this doesn't tell you a lot. So let me share the full story behind my first book.

I live in Vilnius, the capital of Lithuania. It is a small and cozy country in Europe with less than three million people. Most of them are proud that we are one of the top ten basketball countries in the world. If you ever decide to come to Lithuania, I am sure you will enjoy your stay because it is a country that is easy to love! Twelve years ago I had started to work as a sales manager in a company that had been developing software for VoIP business. For those who are hearing "VoIP" for the first time, it is an acronym for *Voice over Internet Protocol*, also called *IP telephony*, or in more common terms: phone service over the Internet.

In the beginning, I had no clue what the purpose of our software was, or why clients would buy it. So as you can imagine, the beginning was hard as I had to learn all this by myself from scratch. The good thing was that I was curious to learn and my boss was patient. After working for some time in this company and talking to clients, I learned that they were using our software to manage a VoIP business. Our software was a VoIP business enablement platform.

Then I thought: If our software is a VoIP business enablement platform, what else is needed to start this business? I began digging deeper and researching this topic. Finally, I understood what was needed to start a VoIP business. I collected much-needed information and created a ten-page guide: *How to Start a VoIP Business.*

It was uploaded to our website and to my surprise, we received organic downloads every day. This showed that demand for such information existed. Moreover, people who downloaded this guide started asking how to do one thing or another. This meant that they were engaged and curious to learn more.

The experience of creating something from scratch that generated demand and brought value for my target audience got me excited. So, I explored more and noticed that there was no book on this topic. I was not sure exactly why no one had written about it. Maybe this topic just wasn't sexy enough. It was very specific, it wasn't trending, and overall there were not that many people worldwide interested in starting a VoIP business.

To summarize this story, my *why* began from the curiosity about the subject of VoIP businesses, which I didn't know much about. Curiosity has encouraged me to explore the relevant material, ask questions, discuss different subjects with more experienced colleagues and clients, and further investigate everything that I have learned. Finally, when I had enough information, I was able to create a short guide on this topic, share it with others, and add value for my readers.

What is your *why*? Do you want to inspire people with your story? Do you want to change their lives for the better? Make them more productive? Teach a new skill? Or maybe you're writing a book not for your readers, but for yourself? There are many authors who began writing a book just because they loved writing or wanted to improve their writing skills.

Writing is a good means for self-reflection, it stretches your creativity, it builds your knowledge, and it is a great way to learn something new. Research has proven repeatedly that we learn the most when we teach others. So write down all the reasons why you want to write the book *now*. Put this list in front of you, whenever you work on your book. Writing the book is grueling work, so knowing and seeing your core reason *why you are doing this* will help you at hard times.

Overcome Your Fears and Take Action

"Each of us must confront our own fears, must
come face to face with them. How we handle our
fears will determine where we go with the rest of our
lives. To experience adventure or to be limited
by the fear of it."
—Judy Blume

We all have fears and that is entirely reasonable. It is okay to be afraid, but you should not let your fears control your life and overcome your dreams. If you don't take action despite your fear, the best opportunities may pass you by and you may regret it for your whole life. Sometimes we fear that we are not enough. Not good enough, not experienced enough, not interesting enough. Have you ever felt this? Think of a time in your life when you faced an opportunity to do or experience something, but you did not take advantage of it because you were not enough.

When I received positive feedback about my ten-page guide *How to Start a VoIP Business* and noticed that there was no book on this topic, I saw an opportunity to turn this guide into a book. But wait...

- I was pretty young (23 years old).

- I had only two years of experience in this field.

- I didn't know how to write a book.

- English is my second language.

- I was working in a full-time job from 9 to 5. There was not much time left for writing.

- The subject of my book was very specific. No publisher would accept it because there are not many potential readers.

- I didn't have any marketing budget.

But I didn't use any of these excuses. The fact that I was able to create a value for my readers with a short guide inspired me to continue writing. You must have heard the famous quote by Albert Einstein: "Try not to be a man of success but a man of value." I wanted to be a man of value and I was confident that I could write a book that would enrich people's understanding of the VoIP business. So I started to take action towards my goal.

However, I had fears. I was afraid of criticism. It took me some time to overcome my fears and to make myself face them, but I was grateful I did it, because the criticism I received was constructive, and I used it to improve my book. Most of the responses that I received later from my readers were positive and I was lucky to receive only one negative review.

You have full control over what you write but you don't have control over what people might say. Positive feedback will inspire you to move forward, constructive criticism will help you to improve yourself, and negative reviews… they will make you feel uncomfortable, but at the same time you will be opening yourself up to the realities of the world: even best-selling authors get negative reviews. However, this doesn't stop them from writing another book.

Now think about this list of excuses that I wrote above. There are many people who have 20–30 years of experience in this field, who are native English speakers, and who have many other advantages over me. But what sets us apart? None of them took action to write this type of book.

Writing a book sounds cool. Everybody wishes they could write a book that would sell well and get five-star reviews. But most of those people will never do a single thing to meet that goal. So overcome your fears and take action. It's as simple as that.

Compare Your Present Self to Your Past Self

I recently participated in a webinar where the USA Today best-selling author Lindsay Buroker shared her experience of writing and self-publishing. Writing is her full-time job and she has sold more than 2 million books on Amazon. I learned that she has already published 60 books and writes on average 7,000 words per day! This sounded crazy and unachievable for me, bearing in mind my current goal to write 200 words per day. If I compared myself to her I would feel a total loser, but I know that there will always be people who are better than me, so I choose to compare my present self to my past self.

We always tend to compare ourselves to others and it's hard not to do that. However, if you want to develop a skill, or achieve a personal goal, you're better off comparing yourself to the "old you." In this way, you can see how much you have grown and what progress you have made towards your goals. This creates gratitude towards yourself and makes you feel good.

It took me five years to write my first book. I finished my second book within a year. My third book was completed in just six months. I enjoy seeing this progress, but what excites me the most is getting feedback from readers about how my book has helped them in one way or another. I am sure this is something that all authors appreciate. So do something today that will make you slightly better than yesterday. Keep track of your progress and compare your present self to your past self.

From Manuscript to $15,000 from Book Sales

The manuscript of my first book consisted of over 56,000 words. When it was completed, I decided to launch a crowdfunding campaign to raise money for publishing my first book. I did preparation work for two months and spent only $160 to make a professional video. That was my only expense. I had zero marketing budget, but despite this, my first Kickstarter campaign was successful. It took one month and I raised three times more than I needed to self-publish the book. I got AU$12,191 (around $8,379) funding from 200 backers, from 35 countries worldwide (see funding graph from Kickstarter below).

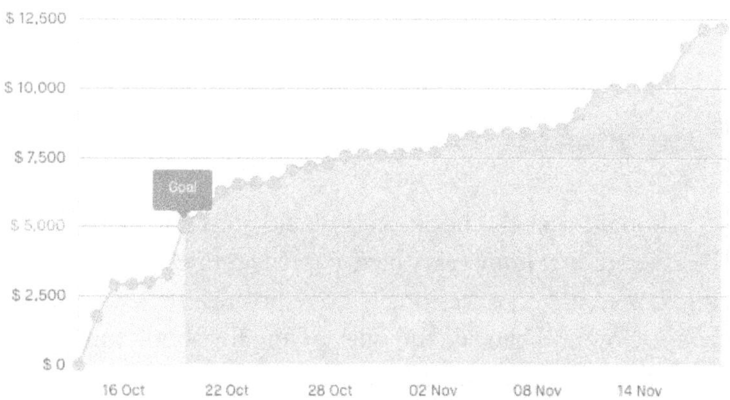

Not all the people in my network knew what Kickstarter was and how to make a pledge, so after my crowdfunding campaign had ended, I decided to continue spreading the word about my book by reaching out to people directly. I contacted people from my network, asked if the book was relevant for them and if so, I proposed to them to pre-order the autographed book at a discounted rate. Using this simple outreach, I was able to generate another $1,837 in three weeks.

By using crowdfunding, I raised more than enough money to self-publish my book, so I hired professional freelancers to do the editing, formatting of interior pages, illustrations, and cover design. Once I received the first printed copies of my book, I signed them and shipped them to my backers and those who pre-ordered the book.

Finally, I published this book on Amazon, where it received more than forty five-star reviews and became the #1 Best Seller in its category ("Telephone Systems Engineering.")

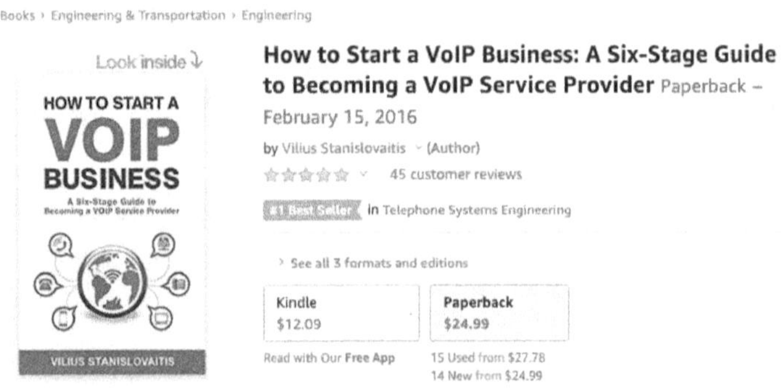

I thought that the book sales would stop after a year or so, but they didn't. Four years have passed and people still buy the book, read it, and occasionally leave positive reviews on Amazon. Below you can see the sales of my first book on Amazon since the day it was published.

Here's the royalty report from my account on KDP (Kindle Direct Publishing). It is Amazon's publishing system that allows you to self-publish ebooks and paperbacks for free and reach millions of readers. As you can see, this book has generated over $7,000 in sales across all Amazon marketplaces. These days, this book generates around $100 per month. There's still a demand for it and I'm even considering releasing a new edition with slightly updated information because some things have changed in this industry since the book was written.

Royalties Earned (What's this?) ˅

Currency	eBook Royalty	Paperback Royalty	KU/KOLL Royalty	Total Royalty
USD	2,363.30	3,921.70	217.57	6,502.57
GBP	160.86	460.17	22.37	643.40
EUR	159.92	285.19	12.71	457.82
JPY	704.00	0.00	645.33	1,349.33
INR	2,180.52	0.00	189.59	2,370.11
CAD	227.83	98.98	16.67	343.48
BRL	103.90	0.00	11.51	115.41
MXN	105.00	0.00	81.16	186.16
AUD	109.90	0.00	3.83	113.73

To this day, I have generated more than $15,000 from my first book *How to Start a VoIP Business*. The biggest piece of the revenue ($8,379) came from Kickstarter and I raised this amount in just a month. Just to compare, it took me just over four years to get the same amount in royalties from Amazon and other two distribution channels (I also used IngramSpark for printed books and Smashwords for ebooks). That's why I think that the book pre-launch and launch are your best opportunities to get the most sales.

I share financial figures to illustrate my self-publishing path, but I didn't start writing my first book because of money. I wanted to share my knowledge and create value for other people. Income from book sales was a natural result because my target audience saw value in what I shared and agreed to exchange their money to get this value.

The income I earned was just one of the good things that happened to me after self-publishing the book. Here are a few other side effects that I received after writing a book:

- People from my industry saw that I was educating others and this helped me strengthen current relationships and establish new ones.

- I gained more credibility as people saw me not only as a sales manager of a company but also as a writer of an authoritative book. This helped to increase the income in my main job.

- Experience with Kickstarter was so positive that it became my second passion. Soon after, I wrote my second book *Your First Kickstarter Campaign.*

- I learned how to write several times faster, how to delegate work to other people, how to outreach to journalists, influencers, and other business people. Those are great skills that can be easily adapted in other areas.

- I decided to enrich my new book by doing interviews with other experienced people in this field. This helped not only to improve the content of the book but also to establish new relationships with awesome people.

- I learned that the book is not the only form of content I can share, so I've published the audiobook and created a video course based on the same topic. By doing this, I gained new skills: talking in front of the camera and editing the video files.

- People started paying for consultations with me.

Now I see that this is just the beginning of something bigger that will help me to move towards my goal of making a living from sharing my experience with others. I'm no different to you. If I can achieve this, so can you.

PICK A SUBJECT: FINDING THE BEST BOOK IDEA

"Either write something worth reading or do something worth writing."
—Benjamin Franklin

What do you feel you could talk about, like forever? If you enjoy sharing your knowledge and experience with others, I am sure there is something you love that you could talk for hours about. Something that you've been passionate about. Something that has left a big impact on your life. Your expertise. Your working experience in the specific industry. Your knowledge about a certain topic. Cars, sports, games, science, business, personal growth, you name it. There are many book ideas and you might get lost among them. How do you select the best one?

The ideal scenario is when:

- you are passionate about the subject you write;

- you are an expert in the field, or at least a long-time practitioner;

- your subject has a high demand and a significant audience cares about it;

- you have engaged followers who recognize you as the authority in this field.

To be honest, you wouldn't need to read this book if you met all the above criteria. Most probably you lack some of these points, but it shouldn't stop you from writing a book. Next, I will share a few stories that will show you how other authors and I chose our subject.

Writing a Book That Didn't Exist Before vs. Writing in a Competitive Category

Nowadays, there are plenty of books about everything. Just think about any subject, enter the keyword on Amazon, and most likely you will find some book about it. If you don't find one, there is a big chance that the subject you are interested in doesn't have enough demand and that is why no one is bothering writing about it. But is it still possible to find a niche that wasn't noticed by others in today's market?

Previously I shared a story about how I wrote a ten-page guide *How to Start a VoIP Business*. The subject that I chose was very specific. Before writing the guide, I researched this subject on Amazon and found books about "VoIP," but it was a broad keyword, and most of those books were technical. However, there were no books about "VoIP business." Why? Most probably because of the lack of demand for that subject: there were not enough readers who were interested in this. Nevertheless, the fact that there was no book about VoIP business encouraged me to write one.

This brings us to an important rule: setting the right expectations about the current demand for your book. How can you evaluate this? Enter the relevant keyword on Amazon and find a few books on this topic. Then click on one of the books and scroll down till you see its "Product details."

Suppose you want to write about how to develop positive habits. A similar book on this subject could be *Atomic Habits* by James Clear. Here are the product details of this book:

Hardcover: 320 pages

Publisher: Avery; 1st edition (October 16, 2018)

Language: English

ISBN-10: 0735211299

ISBN-13: 978-0735211292

Product Dimensions: 6.2 x 1.1 x 9.3 inches

Shipping Weight: 1.2 pounds (View shipping rates and policies)

Customer Reviews:

4.8 out of 5 stars

8,349 customer ratings

Amazon Best Sellers Rank: #61 in Books (See Top 100 in Books)

#4 in Popular Social Psychology & Interactions

#2 in Business Processes & Infrastructure

#4 in Personal Transformation Self-Help

Pay attention to "Amazon Best Sellers Rank: #61 in Books." It shows the overall ranking on Amazon, and it means that there are 60 books on Amazon that are bought more often than *Atomic Habits* and there are millions of books that have lower sales. The higher the ranking is, the more books are sold. To estimate how many books are sold daily and monthly, you can enter the Amazon Best Sellers Rank to Amazon Book Sales Calculator by TCK Publishing.

At the bottom of the "Product details" there is a ranking in specific Amazon categories. As you can see, *Atomic Habits* can be found in three different categories: Popular Social Psychology & Interactions, Business Processes & Infrastructure and Personal Transformation Self-Help. How can we see if the specific category has a demand? Look at the Amazon Best Sellers Rank of the top ten books in that category: the higher the rank is, the more competitive a category it is.

Do this analysis now and check how competitive your category is. If your category does not have enough demand, it will be easier to become a best-seller in your category—but being a best-seller won't bring much value to you because there won't be many people interested in this low ranking category. On the other hand, if your category is highly competitive, it means that there are many readers interested in that subject, but you will have to market your book hard and sell a lot of copies to outrank other books in the same category.

What conclusions can we make here? If you are an expert in one particular field, there are not many choices for you. Whatever the demand for your subject on Amazon, you will have to accept it. For example, when I decided to write my first book, I was able to write *only* about VoIP business. I didn't have any other subjects in mind. So it wasn't hard to make a decision. But if you are an expert in several topics, you can choose what matters to you more: writing the first book on a specified subject in a non-competitive category with less demand or writing a book in a more-competitive category with the hope that your book will outrank other books.

If you are able to write a book on different subjects, keep in mind that people are usually looking for a nonfiction author who is an expert in the specific subject matter. This means that choosing a narrow subject is better than writing about a broad topic. The best nonfiction books are usually those that were written by authors who spent their lives researching a particular issue.

Writing about Something Remarkable That You Have Done

"I became a millionaire at age 36. That was four years ahead of my original goal. My new goal is to have $5 million by the age of 40." This is a quote from the article "What It's Really Like Once You Become A Millionaire" in *Entrepreneur*. This guy did something remarkable that lots of people are dreaming about. Reading a true story about significant achievements, written by a person who is no different from anyone else, is inspiring and engaging. Have you done something remarkable? Have you accomplished something that people told you was impossible to accomplish? If so, share your story with others because there is a chance that you will seize the attention of those who would like to achieve the same results as you.

Even if you haven't become a millionaire at age 36, I am sure that there are still many smaller-scale remarkable endeavors that you have done or could do, that would be worth writing about. One of the most memorable achievements of my life was launching a Kickstarter campaign for my first book *How to Start a VoIP Business*. Kickstarter is a global crowdfunding platform that helps bring creative projects to life. I decided to use this platform to verify whether my book had a demand in the market and if so, to raise enough money to self-publish it. My crowdfunding campaign was successful and I raised 243% of my initial goal. The result was AU$12,191 (around $8,379) and 200 backers from 35 countries worldwide. Later I published this book on Amazon.

The experience of preparation and launching the crowdfunding campaign for my book was truly remarkable for me. I was able to raise enough money for book publishing with zero marketing budget, and I received more support from strangers and people who knew me than I could have ever imagined. After this experience, I got really excited about crowdfunding and Kickstarter. I participated in a few projects as a collaborator, which helped me to practice what I'd learned and make sure it actually worked in other campaigns. I also interviewed more than thirty Kickstarter project creators from different fields, so I could learn their mistakes, tips, dos, don'ts, and key factors to success. Finally, I decided to share this knowledge and experience with others in my second book *Your First Kickstarter Campaign*.

Guess: why did I decide to *interview other creators* instead of writing a book based solely on my personal experience? Because I wasn't confident enough. I thought that my own story would not have enough weight and it might not be remarkable enough for my readers. However, when I share a process that works for tens of other creators, it gives more confidence that the steps I suggest to follow are universal for everyone. This leads us to another book idea—writing a book based on what you have learned from other people.

Writing about What You Have Learned from Other People

There are many people in the world who have done something remarkable. How do their stories reach us? Sometimes we follow them directly, but even more often there is someone else who writes about them. As a result, we learn about those remarkable stories from others: journalists, bloggers, podcasters, talk show hosts, and so on. If you haven't achieved something remarkable yourself, but you love talking to people, there is a great opportunity for you to interview others and share their stories in your book.

Frankly speaking, for me it is much easier to talk rather than write. When I was writing my second book *Your First Kickstarter Campaign*, I arranged live meetings and online interviews with other creators who had launched their projects on Kickstarter. I prepared a list of questions that I wanted to discuss in advance, but usually it wasn't necessary because the majority of interviews turned into regular conversations. Before the meeting, I always asked my guest if I could record our conversation. After all interviews were completed, I transcribed what we had discussed. By using this method, I was able to write my second book five times faster than my first book. Just to remind you: it took me five years to write my first book, and I finished my second book within a year.

This method is perfect if you are a journalist, blogger, or podcaster, but it doesn't mean that you must have a blog or podcast to follow this approach. You can easily find people who are relevant to your subject and invite them to have a chat. While writing this book, I decided to reach out to people who have launched multiple publishing projects, preferably books, on Kickstarter and raised between $10,000 and $100,000.

One of the key figures in this niche was Thornwillow Press that has created thirty-one projects on Kickstarter. Their most funded book was a landmark edition of *Edgar Allan Poe Tales, Mysteries, and Contrivances* that raised $150,915. Thornwillow Press was founded by Luke Ives Pontifell and I reached out directly to him. Here is the email I wrote him:

Hi Luke,

This is Vilius from Lithuania, a small, but a cozy country in Europe.

I've noticed you've launched many successful book projects on Kickstarter. Four years ago I launched my first book on Kickstarter and since then I became really passionate about self-publishing and crowdfunding. Now I'm in the process of writing a new book for self-published authors that will explain how to launch their book on Kickstarter.

Would you be willing to share your experience related to the book launch on Kickstarter?

Vilius

I got the response the same day: "Thank you for your email. Sure. I would be happy to talk with you about this." Then we arranged a Skype call and Luke happily shared his experience with me. Despite the fact that Luke Ives Pontifell was busy with running his company in Newburgh, New York, it didn't stop him from dedicating his time to a stranger from another part of the world.

If I could do this, so can you. Write down a list of people who you would like to interview. Find their contact details and reach out to them. Not only will you have a meaningful conversation and increase your knowledge on a particular subject that interests you, but you will also collect material that you can later turn into a book.

Think about Whom You're Writing For

Before writing a book you must develop a good understanding of the characteristics, qualities, and attributes of your ideal readers. Who will benefit most from reading your book? Where are they in their life? What do they do? What do they dream of?

When I was writing this book, I thought about busy people who have an outside job or a small business and have always dreamed of writing a book one day, or have written and self-published one or a few books, but sales didn't go that well. I know that my readers don't have much time for writing and self-publishing, so all activities that I recommend in the book require just five to ten hours per week. I also believe that people who are reading this book love sharing their knowledge and expertise with others, and have a strong reason *why* they want to write a book.

If possible, try to arrange a live meeting with a few of your ideal readers. If that is not possible, you can schedule an online meeting. This will help you to get to know them better and check whether your assumptions about them are correct.

You will later need this information to figure out where your ideal readers spend their time online and how to attract their interest.

Develop a Habit of Writing Each Day

If you are an aspiring writer, I believe that you already have something in your mind that you want to write about. There are tons of ideas you could write about, but without action, those ideas mean nothing. To be a more effective writer, you need to develop a habit of consistent writing and write a certain amount of words per day. Once you have that skill, you will be able to turn it into any form of content easily. Stephen King, the king of horror, suggests writing 1,000 words per day if you are a new writer. It can be less or more, depending on your writing level, your work schedule, and what you think is achievable personally to you.

When I was writing this book, my goal was to write at least 200 words each working day (I decided not to write at the weekends). I wrote for an hour in the morning before work because I had a full-time job from nine to five. I knew that this was easily achievable because most of us write much more than that in our daily lives by chatting with our friends, composing emails, or posting on social media. Committing to that hour helped me get my third book written, and eventually published.

If writing a book really means something to you, find a way to carve out time for it. Decide the minimum number of words you can write each day easily and schedule the time for it in your calendar. Focus on writing. Do not edit. Do not search for additional information. Just write. However, that is easier said than done.

Many writers often struggle to stay on-task. Sometimes you may realize that what you previously wrote is crap. In such a situation, you may write down a comment about why it is crap and then continue writing. If you keep editing what you wrote or keep searching for additional information to improve your book, you may never finish your first draft. To be a great writer, you must concentrate and focus on writing only. Stick to this plan and you will soon have the job done.

If you feel that you need some external motivation, you could join in with NaNoWriMo (National Novel Writing Month), which is an annual creative writing project that takes place during the month of November, or Camp NaNoWriMo that takes place every April and July. Participants of NaNoWriMo attempt to write a 50,000-word manuscript in a month. This competition helps aspiring authors generate lots of words in a relatively short period.

Another way to keep motivated is to find a writing accountability partner. It can be your friend, a colleague, or a complete stranger who will provide guidance, support, and motivation for you to forge ahead and stay on course with your writing. Together with your accountability partner, you can set your monthly and weekly goals, and have regular discussions about your progress and challenges. If none of your friends and colleagues are writing books, you may find an accountability partner in writing groups on Reddit or Facebook. Here are a few examples:

- https://www.reddit.com/r/WriteWithMe/

- https://www.reddit.com/r/selfpublishing

- https://www.facebook.com/groups/TheWriteLifeGroup

- https://www.facebook.com/groups/20Booksto50k

The only thing left is to take the action. Start writing now. The first step is the hardest one to take. But remember that every book begins with a single step. To become an author, you will have to commit to writing consistently. Only consistent action leads to consistent results. Write, and in the process, you will find out what you want to write about. What excites you.

Only by taking an action will you be able to turn your passion into a book and find out whether the subject is right for you. However, you shouldn't write separated from the world. You should share what you write with your audience and start engaging with them as early as possible.

TEST THE DEMAND FOR YOUR SUBJECT

"The first draft of anything is shit."
—Ernest Hemingway

It took me five years to finish the first draft of my book. That's a hell of a lot of time. Imagine you've spent all that time and energy on your first book. You've revised your manuscript a few times because things change as time goes by. You are finally ready to launch your almost perfect book. This is an exciting moment for you. You finally launch it and… no one buys it. For some writers, this is the scariest nightmare and for others, it is a reality. Some self-published authors even lose money because book sales don't cover their expenses. How can you avoid such a scenario? One way is to test the demand for your subject before writing a book.

Applying Lean Startup Methodology to Writing a Book

I'm a fan of *lean startup methodology* that I learned from a great book called *The Lean Startup* by Eric Ries. One of the key principles that I took from this book is "MVP," which stands for *minimal viable product*. It is the version of a product with just enough features to satisfy early customers and provide feedback for future product development. I hope I haven't lost your attention yet. Bear with me and I will explain how this entrepreneurial principle can be applied to writing a book.

If we suppose that *your book is your final product*, then the MVP should be a *short version of your book* that satisfies the curiosity of your target readers and allows you to receive their feedback or measure engagement. The MVP can be a whitepaper, short guide, case study, blog post, article, short ebook, an excerpt from a book, etc.

Why do you need to do this? It helps you avoid the situation that I described in the beginning of this chapter. After spending months or years on writing without any feedback, you risk publishing something that might be completely irrelevant for people. There is a chance that no one will be willing to spend a penny on your book. Why not test the demand for your subject before writing a book?

In this table, I have compared the main differences between writing with the MVP principles in mind and traditional writing:

	Using the MVP principle	Traditional writing
Writing duration	A few weeks	On average from six months to a year
Feedback from your readers	You *must* get feedback from your early readers	The manuscript is usually shared only with an editor
Changes after the feedback	You can implement changes after the feedback *fast* or you can easily redo your MVP from scratch if there is a need	Rewriting the book from scratch would take too long. If your editor suggests you do so, you will have to spend another six months to a year on this

To summarize, an MVP should be *short,* it should *bring value* to your target audience, and you should be able to *get feedback* from your early readers or *measure their engagement.* If you want to use MVP principles in writing, you should not start with writing a book. Instead, you should start with an MVP that will show whether your *future book* has a demand *now.*

If you follow this simple advice, you will develop an entrepreneurial mindset and this will make a huge difference in your writing career. You will become a more effective writer and will significantly increase your income from self-publishing.

Think about the traditional publishing path. You write a book for a year or two (or five years, if you are as slow a writer as I was with my first book). Then you proudly introduce it publicly and... hope that it sells! The sad truth is that you will be competing with hundreds or thousands of books in the same category and chances that your book will get noticed are extremely low, especially if you are an unknown author without an audience. Whereas by using an MVP, you will spend just a few weeks and will be able to:

- generate an audience before you spend years on completing a book;

- track the engagement of your readers;

- get useful feedback and improve your book.

Why not increase your chances of success, instead of relying only on hope?

Next, I will share a few examples of how you can test the demand for your subject by writing a series of blog posts, articles, or a short downloadable guide.

Write a Series of Articles or Blog Posts

The average nonfiction book runs about 50,000–80,000 words. The idea of writing such a long book is scary, but writing a 500-word article or blog post is not. Luckily, writing a book is just writing a whole bunch of blog posts and organizing them in a more structured way. Moreover, by writing blog posts you will be able to gain a loyal following, and test how your audience reacts to different subjects and what attracts them the most.

We have already discussed that most authors write their book over an extended time and present it publicly only once it is completed. Mine wasn't an exception and also followed this path for four years. Trust me, writing one book for such a long period is exhausting. It was 99% of hard work and just 1% of excitement. But then one thing changed and the last (fifth) year of writing my first book was the most productive.

A friend of mine recommended reading a book *APE: Author, Publisher, Entrepreneur-How to Publish a Book* by Guy Kawasaki and Shawn Welch. Before that, I hadn't read any book on self-publishing, so it was something new to me. In reading this book I learned two important points:

- Being just an author (or a writer) isn't enough. You must be three-in-one: author, publisher, and entrepreneur.

- You shouldn't write separated from the world. Instead, you should start building your audience and start engaging with it as early as possible.

I didn't have my own blog and didn't want to create one because it takes time to build it the way you want, it costs money to pay for the domain name and server hosting, and I wasn't sure if I'd be able to commit to publishing blog posts regularly. However, if you are able to commit to writing consistently, having a blog on a particular subject is a good idea. As I mentioned earlier, only consistent action leads to consistent results. Later I will share two examples of how the blogs of other authors were turned into successful books, but for now I want to get back to my own case.

I had an alternative to a blog: a profile on LinkedIn, where I was consistently adding new contacts related to my main job.

Whenever I got an inquiry from a potential client, customer, or partner, I immediately sent them an invitation to connect on LinkedIn. If I met someone at a conference or an event, I invited them to connect. Within a few years, my LinkedIn network expanded and I had around a thousand connections.

LinkedIn sounded like the perfect platform for me: I already had an audience there, and it was easy to share posts or publish articles that could be seen not only by my connections, but also other LinkedIn members. Moreover, I was able to use the content from my manuscript and see how people reacted to it. So I decided to publish a series of articles, related to the topic of my book.

I first started with one article per week, but after a fourth article, I couldn't keep up this speed. As a result, there was a three-week gap between my posts and because of that, my engagement dropped. I learned that it is better to publish shorter posts with greater frequency. Lower frequency posting didn't attract readers and reduced engagement. Here's the table, where you can see the publishing date, title, length of an article and what result it achieved:

Date	Title	Length (words)	Views	Likes	Comments	Shares
June 11	How Can VoIP Providers Prevent PayPal and Credit Card Fraud	436	862	8	3	2
June 18	Why VoIP Resellers Become Service Providers?	822	1,655	105	18	10
June 25	A Guide to Interconnection for Small VoIP Providers	573	4,122	240	20	26
July 2	The Evolution of Telephony	609	2,586	170	17	33

July 23	Top 7 Trends in Telephony	865	2,652	110	1	25
August 14	What You Should Know About VoIP Callback	820	510	33	2	4
August 27	7 Chapters: The Book About VoIP Business	304	636	67	10	7

As you can see, there is a significant difference between the most and the least engaging article. This helped me understand what topics interested my readers the most and which ones were not so relevant. Moreover, those articles helped me to warm my potential readers up, get them engaged, and slowly introduce my book. At the end of each post I added a line that this article was part of a new book that would be coming soon. That worked really well and some of the readers wrote comments that they were looking forward to the book launch.

Let's look at this series of articles from an MVP perspective:

- They were *short* (on average 632 words per article).

- They brought value for my target audience.

- I was able to measure engagement: the number of views, likes, comments, and shares.

LinkedIn is just an example that worked for me, but you are free to choose other alternatives, such as your own blog, writing a guest post on another blog, Medium, Quora, etc. For example, Nina Amir, author of *Authorpreneur: How to Build a Business Around Your Book*, began her book as a series of blog posts over six weeks. Later she did the same with another book, *Blogging Basics for Authors*, which took her about three months to write on her blog as a sequence of "lessons." She suggests taking these steps to blog a book, in her blog post "5 strategies that turn your blog into a book-writing machine":

- Create a table of contents or outline.

- Break each chapter into post-sized pieces.

- Plan to keep 20% of your content as "unpublished material."

- Write each chapter as numerous 300-to-500-word blog posts.

- Produce a manuscript as you blog.

Another person who has turned his blog posts into a book is my favorite financial blogger, JL Collins. I highly recommend reading his blog jlcollinsnh.com for everyone who is interested in the simplest way to invest passively. His primary goal was to share his key financial lessons with his daughter, but his blog has now grown into an international readership. Later, JL Collins published the book *The Simple Path to Wealth* based on his blog posts. As the author says, readers can find the same information in his blog, but the content is structured a bit better in the book. Even though the same information can be found on the JL Collins' blog, readers still buy the book, which has been very successful even though a few years have passed since it was published.

Create a Short Ebook or Guide

Instead of an article or a blog post, which usually gives condensed information, you can create a short ebook or guide that teaches the reader about something or provides a more comprehensive explanation and in-depth coverage on a focused subject. Ebooks normally contain between 5,000 and 20,000 words, so if you decide to create a short ebook, it's enough to write around 5,000 words of high-value information. If you write a short guide, it can contain even fewer words.

As you have already seen, my first book began with a ten-page guide *How to Start a VoIP Business*. It met all of the criteria that an MVP should contain:

- I created it fast—in two weeks—and it was *short*: ten pages, 3,000 words.

- It *brought value* for my target audience.

- It was able to *measure* the number of downloads.

- I received direct *feedback* from the readers by email.

I wrote for an hour every working day, intending to complete at least 200 words each time. Most days I was able to surpass this goal and I averaged around 300 words per day. To tell you the truth, while I was gathering information for this short guide, I had no idea what an MVP was, or that soon I would start writing a book. The thought about the book came naturally when I received the feedback from my readers.

My guide was *free to download*, and those who were interested just had to enter their email address to receive it. Some of you may wonder why you should give out your guide or ebook free of charge, when you have invested your time and energy to write it. Giving your ebook free of charge in exchange for an email is a great way to attract your target readers and grow your audience, especially if you are a starting author. By having the email addresses of your readers, you will have a chance to create them more value by sending relevant content. Creating value for your followers will make them more engaged and by the time you publish the book, you will have a group of supportive readers who will be ready to buy your book.

If you already have an idea for your book, why not test the demand for it by writing an article, blog post, short ebook, or guide on the same subject? Choose one that suits you the most and *start writing it now*. Write at your pace and make it your daily ritual. Within two or three weeks, you will have your MVP ready. Don't procrastinate on this. Act now and you will see the change. If you get positive feedback from your readers, you will be more confident to write a full book on the same topic.

Don't try to make it perfect, but be sure it contains enough value for your readers.

To test the demand for your subject objectively, it is not enough that your mom and a few close friends press "Like" on your post. Your MVP should be reviewed by your target audience, and the more of these people who read your content, the more objective the feedback you will get. You already know how important understanding your target market is, so next you will learn how growing your audience early will help you build a foundation for your upcoming book.

GROW YOUR AUDIENCE BEFORE YOU PUBLISH

*"You can't expect to just write and have visitors
come to you — that's too passive."*
—Anita Campell

Millions of books are written every year. How can you stand out in this crowded book market? By building an audience of people who care about what you have to say before you publish your book. First-time authors usually don't have any audience when they begin writing. So I think finding a target audience and engaging with it early in advance is the number one goal for everyone who chooses the self-publishing path.

The environment in which your audience can receive your content and interact with you is often called *an author platform*. It takes time to build an author platform and grow your audience. Quite often, new authors start thinking about this just before their book launch, which is too late. Think about the blogs you read and influencers that you follow. How long have they been doing this? How consistent are they with their posts? You will rarely find a blogger or influencer on your radar who is just starting out. Even if you do happen to follow someone like this, he or she is usually an exception to the rule.

You'll need to have patience to build your author platform and if you are just starting out, you will have to test different methods and see which ones allow you to grow your audience in the most efficient way. In this chapter, you will learn more about how you can attract your target readers and keep them excited about your upcoming book launch.

Start with Your Current Connections

The easiest way to build your audience is by sharing your content with those people who already know you. You can start with those platforms or social networks, where you are already active. No need to create an author page or a book page at this stage. Simply use your personal profile that you already have. Previously, I shared an example about me publishing articles on LinkedIn, but if you prefer another platform, that's absolutely fine as long as you have some connections there. However, this works *only* if the majority of people in your network meet your target reader profile. What if your subject is completely irrelevant for your current network? Then you must find where your target audience hangs out.

Be a Part of Your Target Audience's Community

Your first task is to find online (forums or groups on social media) or offline (events, conferences, meetups) communities that are relevant to your writing subject, and in which your potential audience already interacts. Join these communities and make some research. What do people ask the most often? What topics and questions are the most engaging? Write down anything that helps you understand the challenges and needs of your target readers. Doing this will also help you evaluate the demand for your subject with minimal effort.

Once you've done this initial research, ask yourself if you want to be an active member: raise relevant questions, participate in conversations that are already happening, and care about other people's interests more than your own. Building relations with other members and earning their trust requires consistency and takes time, so you'll have to patiently add value for others. Moreover, there is no guarantee that someone will become interested in what you write and will become your follower. I guess you've noticed that I sound a bit pessimistic about this. This is because I've tried this method, but didn't receive any positive results.

When I was writing my second book *Your First Kickstarter Campaign*, I decided to join a few relevant groups related to my niche: using Kickstarter for crowdfunding projects. I created a recurring task on my calendar to answer questions and add value to the community members. I did this for a few weeks, but my patience has soon ended and I decided to discontinue this experiment because my efforts didn't pay back. I spent a lot of time answering questions and sharing tips with people, but in the end, only one or two became my followers. My conclusion was that the majority of the people who joined these communities were hoping to generate some potential clients by sharing their projects, but without proper moderation, these communities had become useless.

However, that was only my experience. During one interview that I was doing for my book, I learned that these results can be completely opposite. The person I interviewed tried a similar experiment in his niche—DIY audio projects. He found relevant communities on Reddit, Facebook and a few specific forums, posted a message that they were looking for beta-testers for their product and within 24 hours, 1,000 people had signed up on their page! He explained to me that members of these DIY audio communities are extremely engaged and supportive whenever there's something new. Even though his project wasn't related to books, this example illustrates how powerful communities can be.

Another successful example belongs to my friend who has recently published his first nonfiction book about his life challenges, and how he ended up working for the Saudi Arabian Crown Prince. Before writing the book he used to share his travel experiences on his social media profiles, and on a special Facebook group that connects people who have a common passion for travelling and exploring the world. By regularly writing posts on Facebook, he saw which posts were more engaging, how people reacted to different types of content, and what post length was optimal. Moreover, in some of his posts, he mentioned that his followers would be able to learn more about that subject in his upcoming book. This helped him warm his audience up and build excitement before launching his first book.

Pros and Cons of Having Your Own Blog

These days it's really easy to create a website or blog from scratch using site builders or WordPress, which is a free content management system. The real challenge is to regularly publish high-quality blog posts and promote them properly. If you already have a blog that has some traffic, that's a highly valuable asset, and you can use it to test the demand for your book subject. If not, think twice about whether you will be able to commit to regular blog posts. It is not worth having a blog if you're not going to maintain it.

The pros of having your own blog are that you can attract potential readers and grow your audience by sharing relevant content. A blog belongs to you, so you have full control over what you write and when you write, and you can change anything you want at any time. If you truly create value for your readers, this will help you build your reputation, and your target readers will see you as an expert in your niche. But all this comes at a cost. Maintaining your blog means that you will have recurring expenses for the server hosting and your domain name. Time to time, you might need to fix the technical issues related to your blog, especially if you decide to change your blog theme, add new modules/add-ons, or simply upgrade your WordPress version. You will have to dedicate your time to writing posts and answering comments. Finally, you will always have to think about what to write next if you want to be consistent. It's a huge job, and often not rewarding enough. We all know some successful blogs, but we soon forget that the majority of the blogs don't attract enough traffic, are outdated, and are eventually closed.

To this date, I don't have a blog because I know that I will not be able to commit to regular blog posts. But that was not an issue in growing my audience. The subject of my ten-page guide *How to Start a VoIP Business* was related to my main work, and it was relevant to our customers and potential clients, so I uploaded this guide to our corporate website. It didn't have much traffic, but it was highly targeted and attracted people that were interested in a VoIP business. As a result, I was able to generate organic downloads every day.

If you work in a company and create content that adds value for its clients, you can use the same strategy. It's win-win-win. You get to validate your idea for the book, your company gets new *leads* (people with an interest in what your company is selling), and your readers get valuable information free of charge.

If the subject of your book is not associated with your main work and you don't want to commit to consistently writing your own blog, you may consider creating a *landing page* for your book and building your *mailing list*.

Create a Landing Page and Build Your Mailing List

A landing page is also called a *capture page* or a *squeeze page*. Its main purpose is to convert *visitors* into *leads*. A visitor is someone who visits your website and a lead is a potential buyer of your book. Someone becomes *a lead* when they express their interest in your work by leaving their email address. By leaving their email address, they agree to be notified about your offers and to receive relevant emails from you.

A landing page has a very simple structure, a responsive design, and is adapted to view from all devices, especially smartphones. Thus it has a high conversion rate for all people who visit it. You can order a WordPress landing page design from themeforest.net for just $39-49 (this is what I did) or use a landing page building platform, such as Unbounce, Leadpages, or Instapage. They provide a complete service, so you can get up and running faster, but they charge you a recurring monthly fee and there's less flexibility compared to using WordPress.

By driving traffic to your landing page, you can build the mailing list of your target readers and later notify them about your upcoming book. A mailing list is the key asset for most authors. After your readers have signed up to your mailing list, you will have the ability to contact them. Email is at least four times more effective in reaching your audience than Facebook because constant changes to Facebook algorithms have resulted in decreased organic reach.

Why would people join your mailing list? Because you promise something that creates value for them—a free gift (freebie) that is attractive and useful for your target audience. In online marketing this is called a *lead magnet* because it attracts leads for your business, and in self-publishing, a *reader magnet* because it attracts new readers for your books. A reader magnet can be a free chapter of another book, a cheat sheet, a checklist, a bonus section, a series of videos (or a short video course), an audiobook, a case study, a whitepaper, or access to a private group. It is used as bait to attract your readers and encourage them to subscribe to your mailing list.

My ten-page guide *How to Start a VoIP Business* was used as a lead magnet (see the picture below) on our corporate website. If someone clicked on "Download Now!" they were pointed to a subscribe form to leave their name and email address. After they signed up, they received an automated email with a link to download the guide.

A reader magnet can also be a free chapter of the book (see an example below). Anyone can download and read this free chapter and if they like it, they can buy the book.

I have previously mentioned that you can create a downloadable MVP. If you have a downloadable MVP (short ebook, guide, whitepaper, an excerpt from a book) you may also add a reader magnet inside it. It should include a link that points to your landing page. Adding another reader magnet in your MVP is important for two reasons. First, this will show you if the person who downloaded and read your MVP found it valuable and wants to learn more. Second, there's a chance that someone who downloaded your MVP might share it with their friends or colleagues. If they find it valuable, they might click on the reader magnet in your MVP and eventually sign up on your website to learn more. Here's another example of a reader magnet in my second book *Your First Kickstarter Campaign*.

DOWNLOAD FREE BONUS

150+ USEFUL TOOLS
TO MAXIMISE YOUR
KICKSTARTER CAMPAIGN

Just to say thanks for reading my book,

I would like to give you this Free Bonus! Enjoy!

CLICK HERE TO DOWNLOAD

(Or go to: https://www.kickstarterbook.com/#bonus)

This reader magnet was added at the beginning and the end of my book. When someone clicked on the button or entered the direct link, they were pointed to my landing page, where they could sign up and get the free bonus. This method helped me grow my mailing list with minimal effort—all traffic to my landing page came from my book on Amazon.

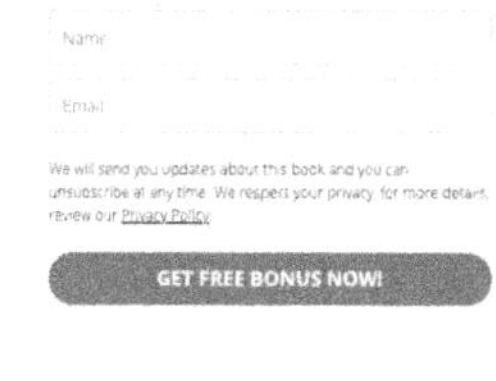

Now you know how to build your mailing list by making your MVP a reader magnet or creating a reader magnet inside your MVP so that visitors can download something valuable by leaving their email address. If you focus on building your mailing list instead of collecting followers on your social networks, you will see benefits. Email is a very powerful and effective communication tool. Social networks change their algorithms quite often to encourage entrepreneurs and businesses to buy paid advertising, and as a result, the organic reach drops significantly.

You can't control social networks' algorithms, but if you have a mailing list, you own and control it. You can freely choose an email marketing platform and if you don't like something about their policy, you can easily migrate your mailing list to another solution. If you choose a proper platform and have a qualified mailing list of people who opted in to your list of their own accord, you can control the engagement rate by creating a compelling subject and providing valuable information in the email body.

Email Platform and Email Automation

Once someone signs up on your landing page, they should start receiving a series of automated emails. For that you need to create an account on an email marketing platform that supports creation of automated emails. For example:

- Mailchimp (has a free plan that includes up to 2,000 subscribers);
- MailerLite (has a free plan that includes up to 1,000 subscribers);
- ConvertKit (has a free plan that includes up to 1,000 subscribers);
- ActiveCampaign (doesn't have a free plan, the price starts at $15/month);
- AWeber (doesn't have a free plan, the price starts at $19/month).

In the first email, express your gratitude for them joining your mailing list and create instant value by giving something for free. The purpose of further emails is to nurture a relationship with your readers, get them engaged, and create even more value. The good thing about automated emails is that you can measure the number of opens, clicks, and responses to your emails and constantly improve them to get better results.

If you want to learn more about this, I strongly recommend reading the book *DotCom Secrets* by Russell Brunson, specifically the chapter "The Soap Opera Sequence" that talks about a series of automated emails. You can also sign up on a few landing pages yourself and analyze the emails that you receive.

Using Someone Else's Website: Guest Post

If you don't have a blog that attracts some traffic and you can't use your corporate website, another option is to find a relevant blog and reach out to its owner regarding the possibility of writing a guest post. Your chosen blog should be *relevant* to your niche and must *have traffic*.

First, you have to do a bit of research:

- Find a few relevant blogs.

- Check if their blog posts are published regularly and if they are high quality.

- Read the comments of the most recent posts. This might show you the level of reader engagement.

- Evaluate how much traffic they have by using Similar-Web. It allows you to compare the web traffic ranking of different websites.

- Subscribe to the blog's newsletter. This will help you to understand the blogger's writing style better and if you reply to some of the emails you get, there's a bigger chance you will get a response.

- Check their social media profiles: how often they post, how many followers they have, and how engaged they are.

Put the information into a spreadsheet and contact the owners of your selected blogs. Keep your initial email short and sweet. Next, I'll share my story of how I reached out to a swimming blogger for a guest post. This story is not related to books or publishing, but it will give you an idea about what you should write, when you pitch the relevant blogger.

At one time, I worked with a startup called Ovao, which was developing a device for swimmers. With Ovao, our goal was to establish a relationship with a specific blogger who wrote about swimming, by creating value upfront. Here's what we did. We took a topic that was relevant to our product and swimming blogs: "heart rate monitoring for swimmers." We researched that topic on Google and noticed that there were several articles, but most of them were outdated. We saw an opportunity to fill in this gap and hired a freelance copywriter to prepare the article. We didn't pay much, around $50, and once the article was ready, we decided to give it away for free to one of our chosen blogs. This is the email I sent to Brent Rutemiller, the editor of the Swimming World Magazine blog:

__Subject__: Brent, here's some swimming-related info for Swimming World Magazine

Hi Brent,

I bumped across your articles in Swimming World Magazine. The reason I'm contacting you is because you are truly one of the most influential people in the swimming world and I'd like to hear your feedback on some interesting swimming-related info that I have.

I've noticed that there are no updated articles on how to boost swimming performance by real time heart rate monitoring.

I'd like to hear your opinion if such an article could be a good fit for Swimming World Magazine?

Waiting for your feedback!

P.S. To make it easier we've prepared a 1,000 word text that you (or your colleagues) could adjust or change (depending on your style) and images for this article.

My goal was to get publicity for the product, but the process of researching blogs and reaching out to the relevant bloggers is the same. I received an answer in a couple of hours.

We are always interested in articles on heart rate as it relates to training.

We can review your article, if you want to send it to us.

Then I sent the article and within a few days, it was published on Swimming World Magazine.

Find your own unique style of this pitch. You may even create a few email outreach versions and test which works better for you. Remember to personalize your message, include who you are, and state what you have to offer. If you cannot find an email for the right person who handles guest posts, you may send your pitch to a general email address, such as info@, hello@, hi@, contact@, and ask if they could point you to the right person.

There's one final tip. Once you get an approval for a guest post, you could also ask if your article can be shared in their newsletter. This will ensure that your post will get more traffic and will be seen by more readers.

Online Publishing Platforms

You may also consider using online publishing platforms, such as LinkedIn, Quora, or Medium. However, you should use this option only if you have engaged in those platforms previously. I think that if you create an account from zero and post an article, it just won't get noticed.

When I started writing a series of articles, I chose LinkedIn as a publishing platform because I had many business contacts there. Even though LinkedIn has huge traffic, I had no idea how many targeted people my article would reach. But overall, it exceeded my initial expectations. Throughout the series of seven articles, I received 13,023 views, 733 likes, 71 comments, and 107 shares.

However, the engagement wasn't related to the number of contacts I had on LinkedIn. It seemed that LinkedIn "pushed" my article and it got noticed by people who were in my second tier of connections. Maybe I just got lucky or maybe LinkedIn algorithms promoted my article to other LinkedIn users in the same niche because my post received a lot of engagement from my contacts in a short time.

Making an Ebook Free on Amazon

Nick Stephenson, author of the great book *Reader Magnets*, encourages authors to start with a short ebook and make it permanently free on Amazon and the other channels. This is exactly what he did with *Reader Magnets*. He created a *short* ebook that contains 4,612 words, which you can freely download from Amazon. Why would someone give his book away for free? Because Amazon is not just an online store—it is a huge search engine and the way books are often found is when people use keywords to search for books. Free ebooks *generate more traffic* and as the book *Reader Magnets* says, you can expect 93-150 more downloads compared to a paid book.

You should care about generating traffic because you are a new author without an audience, and getting traffic to your free ebook will help you to get potential readers. Even a short 5,000-word ebook can create value for your readers and they will see you as an expert of your subject. When you have your short ebook ready, you should put an advertisement (reader magnet) in the front and back, offering something valuable for free in return for a reader's email address. In this way, those who have downloaded your ebook and found it useful will have a compelling reason to give their email address. Otherwise, you will never be able to reach out to your readers and engage with them because Amazon displays only book downloads and sales in the author's dashboard. They don't give any data about who has purchased your book.

I previously stated that I made my short guide about VoIP business free to download from our corporate website, but aside from this, I have never tried making any of my books *permanently* free on Amazon. However, I took the chance of making my books *temporarily* free on Amazon by running a Free Book Promotion that is available if your ebook is enrolled in KDP Select. A quick reminder: KDP is Amazon's publishing unit that allows you to self-publish ebooks and paperbacks, and KDP Select is a free Kindle book program that gives you the opportunity to reach more readers by making your book temporarily free (Free Book Promotion) or running a limited-time discount for your books (Kindle Countdown Deal).

I ran a Free Book Promotion for my first book *How to Start a VoIP Business,* and it was downloaded 205 times. Then I tried to combine a Free Book Promotion with additional advertising in book promotion sites for my second book *Your First Kickstarter Campaign,* and then it was downloaded 1,127 times within 24 hours. It was a part of my book launch strategy and I was able to achieve a really great result—it ranked as the 115th free ebook in the Kindle Store and appeared in the first place in all relevant categories: "Business & Investing," "Startups," and "Crowdfunding:"

Amazon Best Sellers Rank: #115 Free in Kindle Store (See Top 100 Free in Kindle Store)
#1 in Startups
#1 in Crowdfunding (Kindle Store)

But later I found out that ranking place didn't really matter. What actually matters is how many readers who download your ebook eventually become your subscribers. Guess how many of those 1,127 people who downloaded the book actually left their email addresses? Only three people… I was very surprised by how terrible the conversion rate was and thought that maybe something was wrong with my reader magnet or my book. But later I learned that the problem was the *quality of the traffic.*

Those who are "hunting" for free book promotions quite often just download the books and forget about them. When I transitioned my book from free to paid within a few months, I sold 302 copies and received 87 emails during the same period. Even though the number of sales was four times lower than the number of free book downloads, it generated more than a hundred times better conversion rate (see table below)!

	Free	Paid
Book downloads or sales	1,127	302
Subscribers	3	87
Conversion rate	0.27%	29%

To summarize this chapter, your ultimate goal as an author is to create your own platform: a combination of your website, blog, social media accounts, and other media outlets that you can use to sell your books. Start talking about subjects related to your future book at least six months before your book is actually published. We all need to start somewhere, so even if you don't have an audience yet, begin with sharing posts that are relevant to your book subject on social networks or groups that you use regularly. See how your friends and followers react to your posts and engage with them in comments. The earlier you start something, the better you will be at it.

PREPARE FOR A CROWDFUNDING CAMPAIGN

"By failing to prepare, you are preparing to fail."
—Benjamin Franklin

By now you should already know if there is a demand for your book and if your readers (not just your family and close friends) are interested in it. If so, by using your MVP as a reader magnet you should already have some leads who expressed their interest in being notified when your book is launched. Now your goal is to add more leads to your mailing list and prepare for a crowdfunding campaign.

Sell the Book Before It's Published. Yes, It's Possible!

In the previous chapters, we discussed that you need to evaluate whether it's worth turning your MVP into a book by measuring readers' engagement: downloads, likes, comments, and shares. However, the best metric is undoubtedly...*sales*. If you can sell your book before it's even published, that's the best signal that you've done a great job.

Is this possible? Yes! I did it, so you can do it too. Remember, I was young, without much experience, and English is my second language. Despite this, I was able to raise $8,379 on Kickstarter by having just a manuscript of the book. I achieved this goal by spending only $160 to make a video clip. I even created an unprofessional book cover by myself (not proud of it, but take a look at the picture below) as I wanted to validate my idea with a minimal budget.

It seems that the idiom "don't judge a book by its cover" is still true these days. Backers didn't pay much attention to the poor cover I made. Instead, they felt my passion in what I was doing and trusted that I would do my job well.

During the campaign, I managed to attract 200 backers from thirty-five different countries. They helped me to raise 243% of my initial goal and to tell you the truth, it was one of the most amazing experiences of my life! I was extremely excited and wanted to share my excitement and knowledge with others.

The Basics of Crowdfunding: Platforms, Rewards and Fees

There are many crowdfunding platforms in the world and you may get lost in the sheer variety of them. New ones appear, and those that cannot attract a critical number of new projects disappear. But if you want to use a platform that has existed in the market for a long time, has a good reputation and has helped to bring almost 200,000 projects to life, you should choose Kickstarter.

I chose this platform because it is considered one of the most popular crowdfunding platforms with more than six million repeat backers. Kickstarter is a *reward-based* platform, which means that in exchange for backers' money (a *pledge*) you give them some *reward* (in our case, a book).

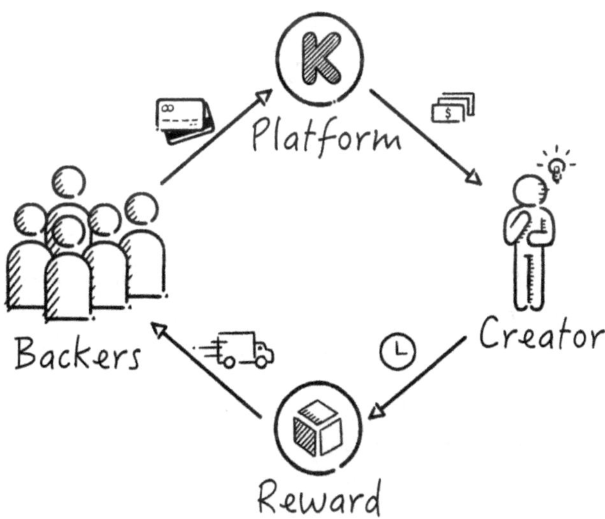

Kickstarter uses an *all-or-nothing* funding principle which means that if you don't achieve your goal, you won't get anything. On the other hand, if you collect exactly what you've set or you exceed your initial goal, you will get all the funds. In most situations, it's better to set a smaller goal that you could easily achieve.

Kickstarter campaigns usually take around one month (the maximum is 60 days). During this time, backers will support your project by making a pledge and choosing a reward. When a pledge is made, Stripe (the payment processor for Kickstarter) stores the backer's credit card details, but doesn't deduct money.

When the project ends and your goal (that you set before launching the campaign) is achieved, Stripe starts processing the credit cards. Once that's done, Kickstarter deducts the platform's commissions (5%), credit card processing fees (3–5%), and transfers the remaining funds to you. Then you will have to do all the work needed to self-publish a book and once it is completed, you will have to deliver your rewards to your backers. When you have fulfilled your obligations to your supporters, you will be able to publish your book on Amazon and other book stores.

Why Is Crowdfunding Important for Authors?

These days crowdfunding has become a major source of funding for creative projects. By using crowdfunding, creators can raise money for their ideas and connect with their community while their project is still in the early stages.

Buying the book on Amazon is very different from pledging on a crowdfunding platform. When people buy a book on Amazon, they expect that it will be delivered fast and in a good quality. Buyers expect to receive instant value in exchange for their money.

When people make a pledge on a crowdfunding platform, they feel emotionally connected to the creator by helping him or her to achieve a goal. Quite often, backers make a pledge not only because they like the product, but also because they want to support the creator. Moreover, backers are more patient because they have to wait until the product is completed and delivered to them, and more forgiving because quite often, creators face new challenges, especially if this is their first project, and as a result, their backers may experience delays in delivery.

If you are a new author who wants to build excitement in your community and have engaged readers even before your book is published, crowdfunding is a great method to achieve this. It is more rewarding for authors than selling the book on Amazon. For example, if you use Kickstarter, which is one of the most popular crowdfunding platforms, the following fees will be collected from your funding total: Kickstarter's 5% fee, and payment processing fees (between 3% and 5%). If funding isn't successful, there are no fees. This all means that you will receive 90–92% of the total funding. If you publish the book on Amazon using KDP, you will get 35–70% (minus delivery costs) royalties for ebooks and 60% (minus printing costs) royalties for paperbacks.

So it makes sense financially to start with crowdfunding and pre-sell your book for your existing audience and all others who will learn about your project during your campaign. When the book is finally completed, you can upload it to Amazon and other distribution channels to reach a new audience. This is exactly what I did with my first book and next, I will share the complete process in more detail.

When Is It Worth Choosing Crowdfunding?

Crowdfunding helps you to turn your leads into backers who make a pledge for your project. The key resource before going to crowdfunding is to have a community of potential backers who might find your project relevant. That's why I emphasized the need to grow your audience in advance in the previous chapter. If you have enough potential backers who are ready to support you, all other steps will be easy. The big question is, how many potential backers are *enough* to be able to launch a successful crowdfunding project? It seems that many creators start doing something yet forget to do the math before taking an action. Doing calculations in advance helps to prioritize tasks and set clear expectations.

Suppose you need $5,000 to self-publish and print the first batch of your book. You set this as a *goal* of your crowdfunding campaign. Then decide what you will give people in exchange for their money (pledges) by creating a list of rewards. Here's an example of rewards related to a book:

- $1 for supporting an author without any reward (you will later learn why this reward tier is important);
- $10 for an ebook;
- $20 for a printed book;
- $25 for a signed copy of a book;
- $70 for three signed copies of a book;
- $100 for a signed copy of a book and a one-hour chat with the author;
- $1,000 for lunch with the author;
- $1,500 for foreign language publishing rights.

As you can see, crowdfunding allows you to be creative and think out the box. On Amazon you can sell your ebook and paperback, and on Kickstarter you can introduce any reward, as long as it is not illegal and is not against the platform's rules. When you launch your crowdfunding campaign, backers are then pledging their money in exchange for some reward.

How many backers do you need to raise $5,000? If we assume that an average pledge is $25, then you will need $5,000/$25=200 backers to reach your goal. The equation is simple:

> Backers x Average pledge amount = Your goal

The next question is, how many leads (potential backers) do you need to collect during the preparation for the crowdfunding campaign (pre-launch) so that 200 of them would become your backers? This is a more complex question that requires additional explanation. The complete equation looks like this:

$$\text{Potential backers} \times \text{Conversion rate} \times \text{Average pledge amount} = \text{Your goal}$$

Conversion rate is the percentage of your audience that was interested in your project who may become your backers. The average conversion rate of successful projects that I analyzed was around 2%. However, you will not know it until you launch a crowdfunding campaign.

Conversion rate depends on many factors, such as how engaged the potential backers are, how well they know and trust you, whether your book fills a niche in a market, whether your Kickstarter campaign page is compelling, etc. You can guess your conversion rate by evaluating the level of engagement with your community and how excited your potential backers are during the pre-launch. But you will never know exactly. I've even seen projects where *none* of the potential backers became backers.

However, if your funding goal is relatively low (for example, $5,000) and the community is really engaged, you can achieve an even higher conversion rate— in my project, it was 10%. I had two groups of people who agreed to be notified about my project. The first group was my friends and a third of them became my backers (33% conversion rate). Another group was my business contacts: clients, potential clients, and partners, who already knew me and had trust in me (9.4% of them supported the project).

I think you can achieve a similar result if the group of early backers are people who know and trust you. However, if you start building your audience from scratch and want to turn strangers, who haven't heard about you before, into your supporters, the conversion rate can be very different.

In the last publishing project, where I was a collaborator, we achieved barely a 0.5% conversion rate by collecting leads using Facebook ads. In the beginning, it seemed that we did everything right. The cover design was eye-catching, the book was unique, the project description was quite well written, and we thought that we had chosen a relevant audience. But I will repeat myself: the truth is that you never know the result until you press the launch button.

In recent years, I've interviewed many crowdfunding creators and their collaborators. Probably the most experienced was Adomas Baltagalvis, who introduced himself as the Facebook Advertising Geek, who was the main advertiser of eight multi-million crowdfunding campaigns. Adomas was responsible for collecting leads by using Facebook ads. Overall, he has spent over $2 million on Facebook ads, helping his clients generate over $30 million in revenue worldwide. He said that if you have a good product-market fit, perfect visuals, and a great project description, video clip, and competitive rewards, you can expect that 3% of people who meet your target audience will become your backers.

As you can see, it can be any percentage, so getting back to our question of how many leads you need to collect during your preparation for the crowdfunding campaign so that 200 of them will become your backers, I recommend creating a few possible scenarios:

1. **Pessimistic**. When you want to turn strangers, who haven't heard about you before, into your supporters and you fail to choose the right audience and warm them up properly, then around 0.5% of the leads will convert, and you will need 200/0.005=40,000 leads.

2. **Average**. When your book has a good product-market fit, you are able to gather the right audience, engage with them in advance, and your campaign is compelling for your potential backers, then around 2–3% of the leads

will convert, and you will need 200/0.02=10,000 or 200/0.03=6,667 leads.

3. **Optimistic.** When your book has a good product-market fit and your potential backers know who you are and trust you, then 5–10% of the leads will convert, and you will need 200/0.05=4,000 or 200/0.1=2,000 leads.

One thing that you *can* control is how many potential backers you must gather to launch a crowdfunding campaign. Personally, *I wouldn't do the crowdfunding campaign for a book if I didn't have at least 1,000–2,000 potential backers* with whom I had previously engaged and to whom my book would be relevant. The number of potential backers could be lower if:

- those are your highly engaged fans and you expect that you will have a much higher conversion rate than 10%;

- your goal is to raise less than $5,000. You can set any goal; it can be a few hundred or a few thousand dollars. The lower your goal is, the fewer leads you will need to have before launching your campaign.

- your average pledge amount is higher than $25. For example, the average pledge amount of the Kickstarter campaign for my book *How to Start a VoIP Business* was around $42 (the price of the book was around $20) and for the publishing project, where I was a collaborator, $280 (the price of the book started at $149). The average pledge amount increases if the price of your book is high or your backers choose your more expensive rewards.

I launched the book *How to Start a VoIP Business* on Kickstarter because I had a community of 2,000 potential backers. It took me five years to make a connection with these people, who later supported my first book. But when I decided to share my story and experience of other crowdfunding creators who I interviewed in the book *Your First Kickstarter Campaign*, I didn't have a community, so I had to build it from scratch. I didn't want to spend another five years to build a new audience, so I set a target to collect 2,000 potential backers in three months. I tried different methods to do that with no budget, but I failed to reach my goal. That's why I decided not to use crowdfunding for my book *Your First Kickstarter Campaign*. I did not want to risk not getting funded, so I went straight to Amazon.

Building a community isn't easy and it takes time. That's why crowdfunding is an ideal place for those who already have a community. But even if you start from zero, you know that there are many different methods to grow your audience that we have already covered in the previous chapter. What if you are not able to build an audience? An alternative way is to find someone who has an audience. You may participate in a podcast related to your niche, reach out to a relevant journalist, blogger or influencer, and so on. We will review all those methods soon and your goal is to test different options and see what works best in your case.

Pre-launch: The Most Important Part of Crowd-funding

Preparation for a Kickstarter launch usually takes around three months, if you prepare intensively and focus on this. But it can also last longer. It all depends on the stage of the idea, the project itself, the goal, and the resources available. The key objective of a pre-launch is to gather a group of potential backers and get them engaged so that they will eventually become your early backers once the project is launched.

Your early backers will give an initial boost when your campaign goes live. This will create a momentum that triggers Kickstarter algorithms (more about these later) and pushes your project to appear higher in the platform's search. As a result, your chances of being noticed by strangers just browsing Kickstarter will increase. Moreover, your project will look like a success because a huge boost in the beginning of the campaign with a solid number of backers is the best social proof that this is something really good!

Below you can see a graph of the most-funded publishing project on Kickstarter "Good Night Stories for Rebel Girls 2" by Timbuktu Labs that shows pledges and backers per day (source: kicktraq.com). You can see a spike in financing and number of backers during the first day. This shows that creators did a good job during pre-launch that created momentum when the campaign was launched.

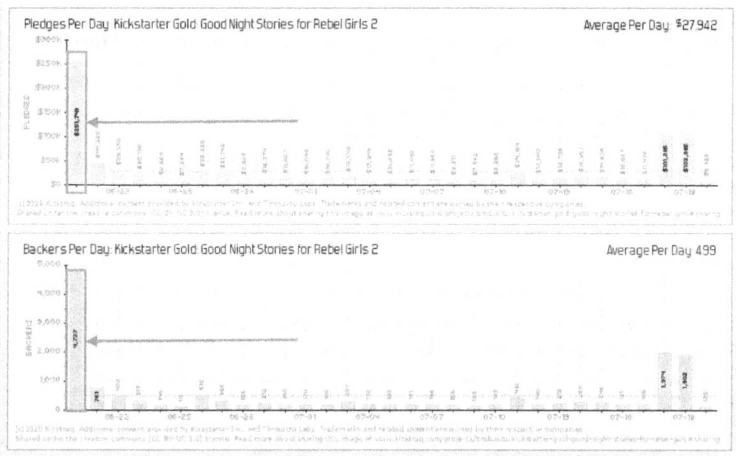

The result that you achieve during pre-launch has a direct impact on the success of your crowdfunding campaign. Kickstarter has a 37% success rate and most projects fail because they didn't prepare at all or their pre-launch wasn't done well enough. Ask any creator who successfully funded their project on Kickstarter and they will confirm that pre-launch is a key to success.

Reaching Out to Your Personal and Business Contacts

The easiest way is to start with those contacts who already know who you are. I usually divide those into my personal (family, friends, acquaintances) and business (people I met in an event or conference, prospects, clients, or partners) contacts. Dividing your contacts in groups is very important because you must reach out to them in a very personalized way using the channel that you regularly use to communicate with them. Let me share how I did this and then you can adapt it to your case.

I used Facebook to connect with my personal network and Messenger to keep in touch with them. I decided not to contact all my personal contacts because I didn't feel comfortable about pitching to those people with whom I hadn't exchanged any messages before. Instead, I selected around 50 friends with whom I communicated more often. Those friends weren't my leads (potential buyers of my book), but they were my supporters. They would support me whatever project I would launch (even if this project was completely irrelevant for them). I'll later explain why their support was important.

I knew that the biggest impact on funding of my first book would be from my business network. I was lucky that I wrote a book that was related to the area I worked in. During my career I've spoken to thousands of people from my industry and had many contacts in my email, LinkedIn and Skype. Overall, I gathered around 2,000 business contacts during my pre-launch. I calculated that this should be enough to reach my funding goal.

Think about the source of contacts that you can use. It can be Facebook, Messenger (I know some people who use Messenger, but don't use Facebook), Instagram, Twitter, LinkedIn, Skype, WhatsApp, Viber, mailing list, followers, CRM (customer relationship management) system, phone book, email contacts, etc. Those who expand their network and constantly add new contacts to their database (whether it is CRM, a spreadsheet, social network, or anything else) have a golden asset.

Currently, I have over 5,000 contacts (and the number is growing) on LinkedIn and this network gives me a big advantage. I can reach out to them whenever I have some new and interesting project related to their industry. If you have a blog with at least 1,000 engaged newsletter subscribers and you write a book on the same topic as your blog, there's a big chance that having just this network will be enough to crowdfund your first book.

The same rule applies if you are a micro-influencer on social networks or have an engaged audience on other platforms. It doesn't really matter which database, social network, or communication channels you use. The most important idea here is to use your current resources instead of jumping on something new.

The next step is to create a message draft for each of your groups. It should be short, personalized, and have a clear goal. It can sound like this:

Hi John,

I'm launching my first book XYZ on Kickstarter next month.

Doing something for the first time isn't easy, so it's important for me to get your support.

Would you like to be notified when the book is launched?

You can simply reply "YES" or "NO."

It's short, personalized and has a clear goal, answer "YES" or "NO." If they reply "YES," add them to the list of potential backers and message them, when the book is launched. If they reply "NO," respect their choice and don't notify them. It's as simple as that.

I encourage you to draft the message by yourself, using your own tone of voice and your own personality. You can make it fun, humble, professional, straight to the point, etc. It should sound like you are writing it rather than a copy-paste from some outreach guru. Also, you could create two different messages, send them to the same number of people, and see which version gets more responses. It's called A/B testing and you can apply it everywhere, where possible, to test different options and measure reactions.

Let's recap this process:

1. Group your contacts by some criteria (e.g. personal and business contacts).

2. Choose the channel that you normally use to communicate with this group of people.

3. Create a personalized message.

4. Add a person's name to this message and reach out.

5. Create a list and add only those people who agreed to be notified.

If you have many contacts in a social network, you can find some tools to automate messages to your connections (just search for "XYZ messaging automation," where XYZ stands for the name of the selected platform, e.g. LinkedIn, Facebook, Twitter, etc.) I've tried automation only on LinkedIn, so I will describe just this example.

To automate messaging (and all sorts of engagements) on LinkedIn, you can use tools like Dux-Soup, LinkedHelper, Ulinc, or Phantom Buster. Just be careful using them as if you send too many messages in a short time, your account may be flagged or banned by LinkedIn. But if you use those tools responsibly and distribute your messages over time, it will save you a lot of time. Phantom Buster suggests sending messages to 80 profiles per day if you have a regular LinkedIn account or 150 if you have a LinkedIn Premium or Sales Navigator account.

Most social networks and email programs allow you to export your contacts (just enter "export linkedin contacts," "export facebook contacts," "export gmail contacts" on Google). If that's possible, you can export your connections (their names and email addresses) and send a follow-up email after a couple of days in case they didn't respond to your first message. Sending mass emails can be automated by using mail merge tools. If you use Gmail, you can try Streak, Mailshake, Yesware, or Yet Another Mail Merge.

I personally use a simple Gmail extension called Yet Another Mail Merge for email outreach and send a maximum of 150 emails per 24 hours. That's a safe limit to prevent your email from being marked as spam. I think two touch points are enough. This shows that you are persistent. But if you cross this tiny line with too many follow-ups, you will be bothering people. No one likes salesy and pushy approaches, so be respectful.

Kickstarter Algorithm. Why Are $1 Pledges Important?

There's a chance that the topic of your book won't be relevant for your friends or business contacts. My first book was completely irrelevant to all my friends. That's why I previously emphasized that they are my *potential supporters* rather than my leads. Let me explain why I still approached my friends, even though I knew that my book was irrelevant to them.

The reason lies in Kickstarter algorithms that pay attention to a few factors: the amount of traffic to a campaign, the number of backers, financing, and conversion rate. The campaign that has raised $1,000 within 24 hours from ten backers will be listed higher in its category than a campaign that has raised the same amount within the same time with just one backer. This means that the more backers you attract, the higher your campaign will appear on Kickstarter search results.

So even if you think that your book is irrelevant for your contacts, ask them to support your project with at least a symbolic $1 pledge and explain why this is important. If there's a boost of new backers in a short time—like if fifty of your friends pledge $1 for your project within the first few hours—Kickstarter algorithms will increase your project ranking and it will appear higher in your category. And trust me, your friends will be more than happy to do something that makes your dreams come true!

Influencer Outreach

If the list of your personal and business contacts isn't big enough, you can reach out to influencers: bloggers, journalists, podcasters, or other people who have an audience that matches yours. Here are a few things you should keep in mind:

- First, your book should be relevant and valuable to their followers. Check their blog posts, subscribe to their newsletter, and read what they share in their social network feed. Reach out only if you see that you can add value to them.

- Second, be prepared to give something in return. As you're writing a book, you can promise a free copy of the printed book (once it's launched) or an early copy of your ebook. Think of the printing and shipping costs of your book as an investment to your marketing that can make a big impact on your book's exposure.

- Third, look for influencers that are not too big to respond to you, but not so small that they would have no impact on the results of your campaign. If you reach out only to big influencers, who get tons of messages each day, you might be ignored as they usually work with strong brands that pay a lot. On the other hand, if you contact a very small influencer, their audience might not make any impact on your campaign. Try to find something in the middle. The best case scenario is if you can find some mutual friends. For example, if you use LinkedIn, it shows mutual connections. Is there someone who can make a strong introduction? If so, there's a high probability that you will get a response.

- Finally, create a list of influencers, sort them by relevance, reach and relationship, and start outreach. (There's a great post on this in Tim Ferris blog, and I highly recommend reading it: https://tim.blog/2012/12/18/hacking-kickstarter-how-to-raise-100000-in-10-days-includes-successful-templates-e-mails-etc/.)

You can reach out to influencers via email or on social networks. Personalize your message, give a compliment, introduce yourself, and explain why you have reached out, how your book can benefit them, and what you need from them. You may also try a shorter version: personalize, introduce, and get straight to the point. Be persistent and make at least two attempts to get in touch by email or social media, but also respect their time and stop contacting them if they don't respond.

Here's a pitch example that I might use to reach out to influencers regarding this book:

Hi {name},

I'm following your blog which is a great source of information and inspiration.

I am about to launch a Kickstarter campaign for my new book that helps aspiring nonfiction writers to turn their expertise into a book. My goal is to reach those people who have an outside job or a small business and have always dreamed of writing their first nonfiction book one day.

Would you be interested in writing a blog post or mentioning this in your newsletter in return for the book?

P.S. I'll be glad to share the manuscript of my book with you to see if it is a good fit for your audience.

People who run successful blogs and podcasts are always looking for new content. If you have something that is relevant to their audience, you will both benefit from this.

Engage in Niche Forums and Groups

There's probably a group or a forum that connects like-minded people of any topic you can think of. Some communities are closed and some are public. Here we'll talk about those that you can easily find and quickly join.

First, you need to find forums that are relevant to your niche. The best way for that is our good old friend Google. Instead of simply entering "[Your keyword] forum" to Google search, I recommend using a combination of two advanced Google search operators: AND and InURL. AND allows you to search for X and Y, and will return only results related to both X and Y. For example, if you enter "Jobs AND Gates," you will get results that mention both "Jobs" and "Gates." InURL finds pages with a certain word (or words) within a URL. If you enter "inurl:apple," you will get results containing the word "apple" in the URL. Forums usually have the following words within their URL: "forums," "forum," "showthread," or "showtopic." So if you want to find a forum that contains your keyword, you should enter:

- Your keyword AND inurl:forums (for example, if your topic is "investing," enter investing AND inurl:forums);

- Your keyword AND inurl:forum;

- Your keyword AND inurl:showtopic;

- Your keyword AND inurl:showthread.

When conducting your research, you will notice that some of the forums are old and outdated. Check a few of the most recent threads and see how active and engaged people are. Select only those forums that are active, have high traffic (you can compare the web traffic ranking of different forums by using

SimilarWeb), and a significant number of engaged members (almost all forums display the number of members publicly).

Building your reputation in a forum takes time. Don't start with a promotional post. When you join a community, first introduce yourself. There's usually an appropriate thread in a forum for this purpose. Use the search function to find questions where you think you can be helpful and engage in a meaningful way: answer questions, share your experience or post a piece of useful resource you discovered. Do everything that makes you valuable to the community. To prevent spam, most forums allow adding links only after you've made a few posts.

Once you have created value for others, you can make a new post and share that you're working on a new book and would like to share a part of it for free with this community. Point interested people to your landing page, where they can subscribe to learn more.

You can use the same tactic with groups. Find them by entering your keywords into the search bar of social networks, such as Reddit, LinkedIn, or Facebook. In this case, pay attention to the number of members in a group and post engagement.

Are Paid Ads Worth It?

Some projects that do not require big funding can be brought to life by using an existing network and other creative methods to attract new backers. If you already have a community, that's great! It means you're almost ready for launch. But most first-time creators don't have a community and building one from scratch without spending money takes time and effort. Moreover, the final result is never guaranteed. What works for others may not work for you.

It is not a secret that most Kickstarter projects that raise $100,000 or more use paid advertisements. It's a faster and more predictable way that you can control and scale. But there's also a big risk—that your investment in ads will not pay back. Especially if the product you want to sell is your first book. I'll explain why.

There are two main strategies for running the ads:

- The first is usually done during the pre-launch and its goal is to get the email addresses of leads and then nurture them with a series of periodic emails. In this case, you point the ad to your landing page, where you capture the lead's email address. When your project is live, you inform your leads that now they can make a pledge. From what I've noticed during discussions with a few creators, such ads during the pre-launch are usually more effective because you have more time to warm leads up and get them excited, and they have a chance to familiarize themselves with your project before deciding to pledge.

- A second way is to drive traffic (ads) directly to your Kickstarter campaign when it is live. Even though it might seem that this method isn't as effective (because you don't have time to warm leads up) as the previous one, it does depend. Different creators might get completely opposite results. For example, there's an agency Jellop Crowdfunding that works with bigger Kickstarter campaigns that trend towards $200,000 funding or more. They drive traffic to live Kickstarter campaigns by using high-precision advertising on Facebook and Google. Jellop Crowdfunding states on their website that "every dollar spent on advertising usually results in $3 to $10 in pledges, even with budgets of tens of thousands of dollars over 3 weeks." This is a really good result because most first-time creators cannot get a positive return on investment with paid ads.

Some math to prove the point: according to Enventys Partners (another crowdfunding agency), the average cost per lead by using Facebook ads is around $1.50 (source: https://artofthekickstart.com/using-facebook-ads-crowdfunding-kick-starter-indiegogo/). When I participated in other Kickstarter projects as a collaborator, I've also found similar results (I'll give you an example later). You saw earlier that the average conversion rate of successful projects is around 2%. Suppose, you spent $150 dollars on Facebook ads and the average cost per lead is $1.50, then:

1. $150 spent on Facebook ads would generate on average 100 leads ($150/$1.50=100).

2. 100 leads would convert to two backers (100*0.02=2).

3. If your average pledge amount is $25, then you would make $50 ($25*2=$50).

To summarize, by spending $3, you get just $1 of income. That's a huge loss! It means that if you want to get a positive return on investment from ads by selling a book for $25, you either need to decrease your lead price or increase your conversion rate significantly. To tell you the truth, that's not easily achievable.

However, using paid ads for books may still work in some cases. In the publishing industry, paid ads make sense if you're a more advanced author and the book that you sell acts like an intermediate stage in the *funnel* that leads towards a higher sale, like more books in the same series, a video course, one-on-one consultation, or a coaching program. In this case, you might sell the book at a loss (and some authors actually do that) because you know that some of your readers will buy your more expensive products or services and eventually this will pay you back.

A good example of this is Russell Brunson, who gives out his book *DotCom Secrets* for free on his website and only charges the shipping costs. A book works as a part of his value ladder: some of those who read his book will sign up to a paid webinar, then some of those pay for private consultation, etc.

That's the bigger picture of an ultimate author platform, and that is for another source. But if you are a first-time author with just one book and don't have anything else that you could sell, most probably you will lose money if you buy Facebook ads. I want to share the most recent experience I had that is related to using Facebook ads for crowdfunding.

I was hired as a collaborator to launch an exclusive book (a huge family bible with more than 1,600 pages) on Kickstarter. Before that, we did a pre-launch and used Facebook ads to generate leads. We were able to achieve an average of $1 price per lead. Most of the leads were from the USA and $1 per lead is considered a good result (remember that the average is around $1.50). We expected that the conversion rate would be around 3% because the design of the book looked really good, we had a compelling story, and the audience that we reached out to looked legit. Moreover, looking at the comments of our Facebook followers, it seemed that they were really engaged. But as mentioned previously, you never know until you press "Launch."

So we launched it and… during the first two days, around 0.4% of the leads from our mailing list backed the project. Then after a few email follow-ups, we managed to increase this rate to 0.5%, but this was still a terribly low conversion rate.

Let's do the math. The lead price was $1, the conversion rate was 0.5%, so the price to attract one backer was $1/0.005=$200. Two hundred dollars to sell one book! You must think that I'm joking, but I am not. It's a true story. Luckily, the average pledge amount was $280 (the family bible was really big and as a result, its price started at $149), so each dollar spent on advertising resulted in $1.4 in pledges. However, it still was a loss for the creator of this campaign. This story shows that either you should have insanely high conversion rates or unbelievably small lead prices.

Of course, you need to make more than you spend. We were not able to do that with paid ads. I tried to repeat lead generation with paid ads later with another book, but the result was still more or less the same. Maybe I'll need more failures in the future to learn something about paid ads and to make this process work. But up to now, I haven't been able to achieve a positive result in Facebook and Google advertising with books. I am keen to learn more about Facebook advertising myself because I think it is a very useful skill if your long-term goal is to build an author platform.

One of the most famous people in the self-publishing industry is Mark Dawson, who is well-known for his advertising course for authors. In one of his interviews (source: https://blog.reedsy.com/facebook-ads-for-authors-mark-dawson-interview/) Mark gave an example, where he's paying $10 a day and getting 30 new subscribers, which works out to $0.33 per lead (that's three times lower than the price we managed to achieve in the example I shared). Once he has moved those acquired leads into his automation, Mark then tracks how well he is able to convert those leads into purchases. He can then determine if he's making a positive return on investment (ROI) on his ad budget. If you want to learn more about this, you can visit Mark's blog at https://selfpublishingformula.com.

CREATE A KICKSTARTER PROJECT

When you have built a qualified audience of potential backers, you are ready to launch your campaign. In this chapter, you will learn what actions you need to do to launch.

Who Is Eligible to Use Kickstarter

The first step is to check if you are eligible to create a project. Project creation is currently available to individuals in the US, UK, Canada, Australia, New Zealand, the Netherlands, Denmark, Ireland, Norway, Sweden, Germany, France, Spain, Italy, Austria, Belgium, Switzerland, Luxembourg, Hong Kong, Singapore, Mexico, and Japan, who meet the requirements below.

- You are 18 years of age or older. People under the age of 18 can launch projects only in collaboration with an adult or guardian who meets these listed requirements.

- You are a permanent resident of one of the above listed eligible countries.

- You are creating a project in your own name, or on behalf of a registered legal entity with which you are affiliated.

- You have an address, bank account, and government-issued ID based in the country that you're creating a project in. Citizens of the EU are welcome to use a government-issued ID or passport from any EU country.

- If running your project as an individual, the linked bank account must belong to the person who verified their identity for your project.

- You have a major credit or debit card (citizens of Canada must have a major credit card).

What if your country isn't supported by Kickstarter? One of the options is to establish a legal entity in the supported country. You can use the Stripe Atlas program to set up a company in the state of Delaware, in the USA—more information here: https://stripe.com/atlas. The setup fee for registering a company is $500 and there are some ongoing costs to run your business:

- Delaware registered agent—$100 per year;

- Corporate tax preparation—packages start at $250 per year;

- Delaware tax filing—preparation is free, Delaware fee starts at $225;

- Bank account (fees, eligibility may vary).

However, if you want to raise just a few thousand dollars, forming a company solely for this purpose might be too expensive. An alternative option is to simply ask a friend or partner from an eligible country to verify his or her identity and bank account during the registration. In this case, your friend, who confirms his or her identity and bank account, will receive payment from Kickstarter if the project is successful. Obviously, you need to trust this person and sort things out about taxes and other financial and legal details before asking for a favor.

When I registered my first Kickstarter campaign, I asked my friend to verify his identity and bank account and it worked well. However, if you don't want to form a company and ask for favors, simply choose another crowdfunding platform, or launch pre-orders for your book through your own landing page.

Confirm Your Identity and Link a Bank Account

If you meet all eligibility requirements, you will have to confirm your identity and link a bank account. Sometimes a project creator and a person who confirms their identity are different people. Quite often this is done if the creator isn't from an eligible country and they ask a friend from an eligible country to confirm their identity. In such a case, the bank account should belong to the person who confirms their identity and they will be the one who receives money if the project is successfully funded.

After filling in all the necessary fields and clicking on the "submit" button you will have to wait for some time for an account to be verified. If for some reason Kickstarter is unable to verify your identity through this process, you may be prompted to use an automated system, which will confirm that you have a valid ID, and compare it with an image of your face, as uploaded by you or captured by your webcam. If there is any trouble with this process, Kickstarter's support team may also step in to help with manually verifying your identity.

Add Project Image, Title and Funding Goal

Next you will have to write a title, a subtitle, a short description of your project, upload an image, choose a category and subcategory, and set your funding goal and campaign duration. All those items are under the "Basics" tab on the Kickstarter project edit page.

The title of your project should be simple, specific, and memorable. Take a look at the titles of ten successful Kickstarter projects in your category and learn how they differentiate from others. Keep in mind that Kickstarter search looks through words from your project title and short blurb (description) so make them representative of what you're creating.

The short blurb has a limit of 135 characters. If you manage to reach a higher ranking in your category or other Kickstarter search pages ("Recommended for you," "Trending," or "Projects we love"), the short blurb will appear with your project image. Then, if someone clicks on your project, they will see this short description just below your project title.

The project image is the first thing that visitors see when they open your project page on Kickstarter. The image has to be high resolution (technical requirements: at least 1,024x576 pixels, 16:9 aspect ratio, file limit is 200MB, supported formats are JPEG, PNG, GIF, and BMP), representative of what you're creating, and it must stand out from other projects, accentuate your uniqueness, and raise interest in a random visitor, so they would like to learn more about your project. Kickstarter recommends providing clean pictures without additional elements (banners, badges, or extra text), so the visitor will not be distracted by excess information.

If you use Kickstarter to raise funds for your book, your main category will be "publishing." You may also choose a subcategory, which is optional, but it allows you to put your project in a certain niche. Currently there are the following sub-categories under publishing: academic, anthologies, art books, calendars, children's books, comedy, fiction, letterpress, literary journals, nonfiction, periodicals, poetry, radio & podcasts, translations, young adult, literary space, and zines. For those who don't know, a zine is a self-published, non-commercial print-work that is typically produced in small, limited batches. Zines are a great way to publish your own art, poems, writing, musings, and other creative work.

When a backer wants to explore projects on Kickstarter by category, they can review all projects in that category or only a certain subcategory. If you choose a subcategory, your project will appear under both the subcategory and the parent category. Personally, I think it's worth choosing a subcategory, as you will give a chance for your project to be found by a backer who narrows down their search as much as possible to find the kind of project they want to see.

Your funding goal should be low, but realistic. Set the minimum amount you need to make what you promised and to fulfill all rewards. Calculate your self-publishing costs: editing, formatting, interior page and cover design, printing, packaging, and shipping. Don't forget to take into account the Kickstarter platform fee, credit card processing charges, and taxes. Once you've launched the project on Kickstarter, you will no longer be able to adjust the goal.

The funding duration on Kickstarter can last from one to sixty days. Kickstarter has done some research and found that projects lasting any longer are rarely successful. Even though it sounds logical to choose the maximum duration, I wouldn't recommend doing so for two reasons. First, the longer the project lasts, the harder it is to keep up the excitement for backers. Backers will simply get bored. Second, if someone backs your project early, they will have a longer timeframe to change their minds and cancel their pledge. I recommend setting your campaign at 30-35 days. Campaigns with shorter durations create a psychological sense of urgency around your project, which results in higher success rates.

Create a Project Video

The video is one of the most important parts of the campaign. Most users prefer to quickly watch a video instead of reading the project description. Videos are not required to launch the project, but Kickstarter statistics show that campaigns with compelling videos have double the success rate of projects without videos.

To keep your viewers' attention, the video should last up to two to three minutes. The first thirty seconds are the most important, since they determine if someone will finish watching the video or turn it off. Once you launch the project, in the creator's dashboard you will see statistics showing how many times the project video was played and what percentage of those plays were completed (see the image below).

If your video is too long, a high percentage of viewers may not watch your video to the end. To grab the viewers' attention and really connect with them, you have to maintain intrigue throughout the video. In the end, there should be an encouragement to act further—to support your project or share it with others.

You can find inspiration and new ideas by watching videos presented by other Kickstarter creators. Just do not overdo it and do not copy everything. Be yourself: if you feel better when you are serious, be that way, and if you have a great sense of humor, show that. You should convey authentic emotion in your video, so be sincere and vulnerable. Being vulnerable is not a weakness. It's actually a strength because you are not using any kind of a mask to hide the real "you."

Tell your story: what encouraged you to take on this idea? What problem did you encounter? Nowadays, it is said that it's more important *why* you are doing it and not *what* your product does. For everything to go smoothly, you will have to write a script for the video—what will be said and shown. Rarely will you be able to do it successfully from the first take, so dedicate some time for testing and corrections. Rehearse the speech with your friends—the more often you say it, the better you will do in the final recording of the video. If you do not feel comfortable on camera, you do not have to be filmed. There are a lot of successful videos in which the creators do not even appear.

Add a Project Description

A book description is one of the key elements that determines if the reader will want to buy your book. Most writers struggle with that because they are not always good with marketing and think that the description is just a quick summary of the book. However, it's rather like an ad that encourages the reader to take the next step that eventually leads to purchasing the book. Think of your project description as the "sales page" for your book.

The description should be short, simple, easily readable, and most importantly—it should intrigue the reader. The first two sentences of the description should hook your readers. Visuals are especially important, so include images: infographics, photos of your manuscript, illustrations (if you have them), user reviews, and other visualizations.

There's a slight difference between descriptions of nonfiction and fiction books. Nonfiction descriptions often include bullet points to outline what readers will learn after reading the book and some facts that demonstrate the author has experience in this field. When describing a fiction book, think about it as a movie trailer that is catchy and leaves the reader wondering what happens at the end.

To get some inspiration, read descriptions of other book projects on Kickstarter. Try to think about what makes them intriguing and what hooks authors use that catch your attention. Then write your own description, improve it based on other examples that intrigued you, and share it with someone who can give you feedback.

Create Motivating Rewards

People back projects on crowdfunding platforms for two main reasons. Firstly, they want to be a part of the community that supports creators to realize their ideas. But even more important is what backers will receive in exchange for their financial support. That is why you should create motivating rewards for your backers.

The reward title and description should be short and clear. Make a bullet list if the reward consists of a few items. Display reward illustrations in the project's description page, so the backers can see what they will receive.

When setting a delivery date, be pessimistic, not optimistic, and add a few extra months to what you have initially planned. Most first-timers on Kickstarter experience delays in creating their product and if they don't deliver on time, they will disappoint their backers and may receive negative reviews and lose their trust. Don't make that mistake and set more pessimistic expectations in advance. If you manage to deliver earlier, you will just make everyone happy!

Keep in mind that when a backer chooses a certain reward, after you have launched your project, you will not be able to edit it. However, if no one has selected this reward yet, you will be able to make changes or remove it completely. You will also be able to create new rewards during the campaign.

How Much Money Will People Pledge to Your Project?

Previously, we used an average pledge amount to calculate how many backers you need to fund your project. The truth is that every backer is different—some can only give a couple of dollars, others several dozen and others several hundred, and there may even be a person willing to donate several thousand. If you are a first-timer on Kickstarter, it will be hard for you to predict how much money your supporters will be willing to spend on your project. That's why it's good to introduce different reward levels so that backers can easily choose the reward value and a price ratio acceptable for them.

Before launching my campaign, I expected that people would be either supporting me with a symbolic pledge of $1 or would buy one book for $20. But as I already repeated a few times in this book, you never know until you press."Launch." The highest pledge amount for my project on the first day was $349, on the third day, $557, and on the fifth day, $1,095. Later in this chapter, I'll explain what I promised (and what you can do too) in exchange for more money.

Donation without a Reward

The Kickstarter platform creates these lowest-tier rewards automatically. They will not have any direct influence on your funding goal, since the sums are symbolic, but they will allow you to quickly increase the number of backers.

The more backers that support the project in a short time, the bigger the chance that it will appear higher in your category in the Kickstarter search pages. This may attract organic backers who are reviewing projects in a certain category.

As mentioned previously, donations without a reward are a great option for all your friends, family members, and anyone else who doesn't actually need your book, but would still like to support you.

Transforming Your Book into Different Formats

What's great about writing is that you can easily transform that into different formats. We've previously discussed that you can start an MVP with a series of blog posts and later turn them into an ebook. Then you can create a printed version of this book, narrate an audiobook, or make a video course. Content is the same, just the format is different. And that's great because with minimal effort you can reach a broader audience.

I had a digital copy of my book in PDF format as a reward, but I hadn't thought about an audiobook or video course. However, that's something that I have implemented with my second book *Your First Kickstarter Campaign*, which is now available as an ebook, paperback, audiobook, and an extensive video course.

Challenges and Great Emotions with Printed Books

To tell the truth, I was very happy with digital rewards, because I could send the book in PDF format to my backers very quickly, with minimal expenses and without any problems. But when I was sending the printed books, I had to break a sweat: sign each book, purchase suitable packaging, calculate the total weight of the package, enter the addresses of all backers into a system, print a list, and cut out and attach the backer addresses to the appropriate packages (because each book had a dedication to a specific person).

Additionally, some of the packages never reached their addressee and were returned for various reasons. So I had to work quite a bit when sending packages to countries such as Ethiopia, Nigeria, and Kosovo. The shipments were usually returned or, even worse, simply got lost and did not reach their addressee. Although shipment registration and insurance might help to avoid such losses, in my case, it was cheaper to lose a couple of the shipped books rather than register and insure all shipments. If I could turn back the clock, I would likely have limited project support to certain countries, or I would have registered and insured only those packages that were sent to more risky destinations.

Even though I struggled with delivery and digital rewards are really easy to manage, I still prefer to have paperback books. Let me explain why. When I got my first proof copy that I could hold and feel, I experienced a feeling of accomplishment. It's an unbelievable feeling and if you haven't experienced it yet, I'm certain that you will enjoy that! Moreover, some readers from different parts of the world sent me photos of themselves holding the book. When you read a positive review, it's great, but when you can see a picture with a person holding your book and smiling, it's just amazing! All those emotions pay back the struggle related to printing and shipping books.

Finally, the delivery of printed books is a one-time job. Once you're done with fulfilling Kickstarter rewards, you can open an account on KDP as we discussed previously. KDP prints your book on demand and subtracts your printing costs from your royalties. That means you don't have to pay any costs upfront or carry any inventory. You can also order proofs and author copies of your paperbacks on KDP.

Setting the Reward Price

If backers choose donation without a reward, they can enter any amount. In all other cases, you should set the price. To do that, you need to research other comparable books so that your book won't be too high or too low compared to your competitors. Analyze a few similar projects on Kickstarter and check book prices on Amazon in your category.

Once you've determined the price of your book, you can start creating rewards. There's one thing though. Since crowdfunding backers are taking a risk when they support the project and wait for it to be delivered to them, it is expected to have a lower price than the final retail price of the book.

I actually followed this strategy because I was scared that if I made the same or a higher price on Kickstarter than on Amazon (once the book was officially launched), backers would be angry at me that I had been unfair. But now I have a different opinion. I don't think that you should necessarily offer a book at a lower rate than your planned retail price. However, you need to explain this for your backers (and yourself). Here's how Seth Godin did this in his Kickstarter campaign for his book *The Icarus Deception*:

> *I can't possibly sell this to you cheaper than an online bookseller, but it's here as an option for those who prefer to get just one copy mailed to them. I'm hoping that you will buy the four pack instead because it's such a good deal. Also includes access to the preview digital edition.*

In this example, Seth is being transparent with his audience and tells them that the book won't be sold cheaper than an online bookseller. This didn't stop backers from supporting his project. His backers got an emotional value that they were a part of a community supporting a great cause. You can't get this feeling by buying the book on Amazon. Moreover, early backers received the book before it became available on Amazon and in bookstores. That's undoubtedly important for some people.

You can also think about what value you could add to your book that people won't get from online booksellers. It could be a nicely packaged book, presented as an exceptional gift, an autographed book with a personal dedication, a book with an exclusive cover, etc. By adding more value, you can create rewards at a higher price.

Scarcity Principle and Early Bird Rewards

Previously, I explained that you can increase your project ranking on Kickstarter by getting a spike in financing and the number of backers in a short time. You must do this from the moment you launch. That's the reason why you gathered those leads and asked your friends to support your project. I'm sure that some of those people will make a pledge on the first day just because they really want to help you. But if you want to convert people who don't know you into backers, you should be aware of what psychological triggers encourage people to make a purchase.

You probably have heard that the decision to buy is made subconsciously, and then we justify our emotional signals to buy with logical reasons. There's a great book by Robert Cialdini, *Influence: The Psychology of Persuasion*, that describes the main principles of persuasion: reciprocation, authority, commitment and consistency, social proof, liking, and scarcity.

Simply put, scarcity means that when there is a limited quantity of valuable things, people start wanting them more. Have you ever seen a warning "one room left" when browsing for a place to stay or "one seat left" when searching for a flight? This is a good example of scarcity. It is designed to pressure holidaymakers into making an immediate purchase.

You can use the scarcity principle by introducing early bird rewards in your Kickstarter campaign. It is a limited amount of your products (books), offered for a discounted price to the most loyal backers who joined your email list or expressed their interest in your project in another way during your pre-launch campaign. The number of early bird rewards is limited (50, 100, 200 units, or similar) and you can create several levels of them: for example, 50 units for $15: super-early bird or 50 units for $20: early bird.

Having a limited number of books for a lower price creates an urgency for potential backers to support the project as early as possible. Imagine that you created an offer: 50 units of your books for just $15. Suppose early backers have already pledged for 48 units and just two books are left. Some random visitor notices your project and sees that just ten hours have passed and only two items of your book are left at a discounted price. Suddenly they start feeling that those two items will soon be gone and they will lose this opportunity. This creates pressure and now they feel that they must take this chance. To justify their actions, they read your project description and find reader reviews. Now they have a social proof that someone else liked your book and they're not alone. They're finally convinced both emotionally and rationally to back your project.

The Most Expensive Rewards

The final reward level, which resides at the bottom of the *Kickstarter* reward list, is the most expensive reward. These are usually related to a unique personal experience or something special that the creator can offer.

When I was creating the rewards on Kickstarter for my book *How to Start a VoIP Business*, I estimated that most people would support the project by choosing one unit of the book. Then I calculated that I would need 200 such backers to reach my goal. After having analyzed other projects related to books, I decided to create more expensive rewards, just in case. One of them was $295 for the option to leave a review on the back cover of the book.

I was shocked when the first supporter not only chose the reward for $295, but donated much more—$369. And that was not even the best news. A day later, another supporter chose the $295 reward, but donated twice as much—$590! Even though this reward was limited to five, there was more demand for it than I had expected initially. Shame that the space on the back cover of the book was limited. And that was not the end of it…

On the fifth day of the project, I was blown away, because one backer bought the most expensive reward for $1,095! Here's the description of this reward:

> *EXPERIENCE. You will get an exclusive day tour with me in Vilnius (Lithuania). We'll visit all the awesome places and you will get dinner in a very special location.*
>
> *Location: Vilnius (Lithuania) & surrounding areas.*
>
> *Travel and accommodation costs are not included.*
>
> *+ SIGNED copy of the book, PDF copy of the book AND your name in the book as gratitude for being a backer*

The person who chose this reward wasn't a stranger. I knew him from my main job. A funny fact was that we have invited him to come to Vilnius a couple of times before, and it turned out that he would arrive here only when he had made a generous donation for my project. When he arrived in Vilnius and we were having lunch, I asked him why he made this decision to support my book. He explained that he saw the passion in what I was doing and just wanted to make a pledge towards my goal. You never know what a supportive environment you have around you until you ask for help.

Rewards related to the unique experience aren't something I created and I'm not the only one who has succeeded with them. I'm sure you will notice this yourself when analyzing other book projects. Why do people choose those rewards? Because they feel the passion of the creator and want to make an impact by supporting them in their journey.

I actually got so excited with high-level rewards that during the campaign, I decided to create the most expensive reward tier—exclusive distribution rights of the book in any other language except English. I wasn't able to sell that, but there were a few people who were interested.

Rewards of My Campaign

Below is a table that shows the list of rewards I used for my campaign. You may notice that the reward price multiplied by the number of backers may not always match the number of total pledges. There are two reasons for that. First, most of the rewards involve shipping, which has a separate price and you can set it by country. Second, by choosing any reward backers can increase their pledge, and many backers did that in my campaign.

Reward	Price (USD)	Total pledges	Number of backers
Donation without a reward	$1 or more	$308	38
Printed book (early bird price)	$17	$865	40
Printed book (regular price)	$21	$2,303	92
Two books	$41	$588	12
Five books	$96	$704	6
One hour consultation + a book	$119	$486	4
Ten books	$188	$425	2
Review on the back cover	$295	$1,605	5
Day with an author	$1,095	$1,095	1

Overall, during my Kickstarter campaign, I sold 216 books. If we assume that the average book price was $20, it should have generated $4,320 in income. But I actually received almost twice more—$8,379. Why? Because of creative rewards that I introduced. Now you understand the importance of this part, so take this opportunity and dedicate some time to brainstorm different ideas for your rewards.

Submit the Project for Review

After you finish setting up your campaign, you have to submit your project for review. Kickstarter recommends allocating at least two to three business days for the review process, but on average, it's done in thirty hours for most projects.

Once Kickstarter confirms that you are good to go, you can share the project preview link with an editor who could go over your page with a close eye for typos and with your friends and colleagues who could have a fresh look and provide valuable feedback. Don't be surprised if there are mistakes that you just don't notice, simply because you have looked at the same text too many times.

Those who have a project preview link can post their suggestions in a comment field. Pay attention to the fact that these comments are public and will be seen by everyone using a project preview link.

Once the project is launched, the preview link will be automatically redirected to the live campaign and all comments written by those who reviewed your project won't be visible.

LAUNCH A KICKSTARTER CAMPAIGN

Running the campaign isn't so hard if you've done your pre-launch strategy properly. By now, you should have a list of potential backers, influencers who agreed to share your project with their followers, and your family and friends who have agreed to back your project with at least a symbolic donation. If you have that ready, it's time to make a next step: press the "Launch" button to make your project public and accessible to the entire world.

The Launch Day

This is probably the most exciting and important day of your campaign. It's the day when your project becomes public and you will finally see the reaction from your potential backers. Here's the main list of things you need to do during the first minutes after launching your campaign:

- Send an email to potential backers who opted in to the mailing list.

- Send private messages to your friends, family, and colleagues through the same communication channel that you use with them regularly.

- Contact influencers and tell them that your campaign is launched.

- Make a post on social media (your personal profile and the project profile) and your blog (if you have one).

- Post to relevant forums, social media groups, and other websites where you've previously engaged with the community during the pre-launch. Don't spam.

- Redirect the traffic from your landing page to your Kickstarter page. Before launching, your site has been used to collect leads, and now it should point all site visitors to your campaign.

- Add your pre-written list of frequently asked questions (FAQs) onto the project page. Kickstarter allows you to add an FAQ only once the project is live, so prepare it in advance and when the time comes, just copy and paste it.

All of the above tasks should be prepared in advance. You should create the necessary texts, emails, and posts on social media and schedule them. By doing this, when your campaign is live, you won't need to worry and stress yourself on the launch day.

Communication with Backers

After having launched the project, you will receive emails, messages, and comments from potential and current backers. Review them constantly and reply as quickly as possible. You can also communicate with your Kickstarter audience by posting project updates. That is like a mini blog for the most important events and information related to your project.

Potential backers may wonder whether to support your project or not. Most of them quietly consider this decision within their thoughts, while just a few will write messages or public comments related to their doubts. That's the perfect chance for you to learn about their concerns and react appropriately.

It's especially important to act quickly, while their wish to make a pledge has not yet passed and you can still influence their choice.

Sometimes backers cancel their pledge before your campaign ends. That's why I recommend sending a private message (you can simply say "Thank you for your support") through Kickstarter to everyone who has just become your backer. This way, you will be able to contact them privately again if they decide to cancel their pledge, see their reason for cancellation, and provide the right argument to retain their pledge. If you haven't sent a message to a backer before they cancel their pledge, the possibility to contact them will disappear from your dashboard.

If you receive a lot of questions, you can optimize the answers by using TextExpander. This allows you to quickly insert "snippets" (email addresses, signatures, text chunks, images, etc.) as you type, using a simple keyboard shortcut, or custom abbreviations. It saves your time without typos and copy/pasting.

You can post a few updates during your campaign and you can select if they will be seen publicly or if only your backers will see them. Here are a few ideas for when you can post a comment:

- You reached a significant number of backers (100, 200 or 500).

- Kickstarter mentioned your project on their newsletter or social feed, or selected it as the "Project We Love."

- You raised 50, 100, or 200% of your goal.

- The press covered your project (you can also highlight this in the project description page by mentioning media outlets that wrote about you).

- A well-known influencer shared something interesting about your project.
- You received a great piece of feedback from your backers.

You may also share your excitement during the campaign. People support your project not only to receive their reward but because they also feel emotionally attached to what you do, so sharing your emotions shows your vulnerability and creates a stronger bond with your community.

Ask your closest backers who supported your campaign to share their feedback in the comments section of your project. Positive public reviews will increase the credibility of your project.

Upselling

This is a relatively old sales technique that allows you to make a more profitable deal. By upselling, a seller induces the client to purchase more expensive items, upgrades, or other add-ons. On Kickstarter, a backer can only select one reward and during the campaign, they can upgrade or downgrade their pledge. So the only way to increase your profit per backer is to encourage upgrading to a more expensive reward.

The first option is upselling within the same reward. If you have the main product and some add-ons for it, you can simply inform your backers that if they want an add-on item, they must increase their pledge by the price of the add-on. For example, the main product is your book that costs $20, and by adding another $10, your backers could get a signed copy of your book in a nice gift package. You can inform your backers about this in two ways—a private message or an update.

To send a private message, go to your project page, click on "Backer Report," select a backer, and write something like this: "Hi [Name], would you like to get a signed copy of the book in a nice gift package? If so, just add another $10 to your pledge." At the end of the message, you may add a link for them to edit their reward, which looks like this: https://link_to_your_project **/pledge/edit**). When a backer clicks on this link, they will automatically be directed to the page where they can increase their pledge. You can also inform backers by posting an update, but personalized private messages are more effective.

Another way to upsell something is to create new rewards, like a hardcover version of a book, and encourage backers to choose them instead of their old reward. In this case, take your project link and then add **/pledge/new/** to the end of the link.

Get Traffic from Kickstarter

Kickstarter has a huge volume of visitors. That's one of the reasons why most creators choose this platform. They expect that at least a small part of organic traffic from Kickstarter will back their project.

Kickstarter has a large variety of options to filter projects for their users: "Recommended for You," "Projects We Love," "Saved Projects," "Trending," "Nearly Funded," "Just Launched," "Backed by People You Follow," and "Everything." In addition to this, users can select projects in a certain section, category or location. However, while exploring projects, people pay more attention to those campaigns that appear in the first search results page. So the goal of each project creator is to try to keep their campaign as high as possible on Kickstarter's rankings.

Projects that are marked as "Projects We Love" are determined by a special team on Kickstarter that reviews and selects projects they like, whereas the "Trending" and "Popularity" rankings are done by Kickstarter's inner algorithms. The default sort of "Advanced Discover" search is called "Magic." As Kickstarter explains, it displays a rotating cross-section of compelling projects by surfacing a mixture of "Projects We Love" and what's popular.

What Does the Kickstarter Team Say about Organic Traffic?

Even though I would recommend being pessimistic and not to expect any backers from Kickstarter, I was still curious myself to learn whether there were some statistics on how many backers came from organic Kickstarter searches. I searched for the answer in the public Kickstarter statistics (see https://www.kickstarter.com/help/stats). Sadly, I did not find the information I was looking for, so I decided to contact the platform's team. I received this answer:

> *When it comes to getting new backers, we see time and time again that getting the word out through your own existing networks is the most effective. Many people browsing Kickstarter do look around for new projects to back, but the majority of the people who find and back your project will be friends, friends of friends, or fans of the work you do.*

It's a very general answer. Kickstarter states that the majority of backers will be your own crowd and only a small group of people who browse Kickstarter and look around for new projects might support your campaign.

Once your campaign is live, in the project's dashboard you will be able to see how much money was pledged via Kickstarter. You may think: "That's the number that shows organic traffic!" However, it's not accurate because not all people will back your project instantly after you send them a link. Some of them may need some time to think and some will remember you after a certain time. Even though they knew about your project earlier, whether from you, your ads, or another source, they may later enter your project name in Google or the Kickstarter search, find your campaign, and make a pledge. As a result, such backers will be shown as those who pledged via Kickstarter, even though they originally learned about you from somewhere else.

"Projects We Love" Badge

There's a dedicated team on Kickstarter that is constantly looking for exceptional projects. They are reviewed manually and those that really stand out as particularly compelling are marked with the "Projects We Love" badge. This is universally considered a good thing because your project then appears higher in default Kickstarter searches, sorted by "Magic."

There's no secret recipe for how to get featured in the "Projects We Love," but here are a few general tips that you can follow in order to have the best possible chance of catching the eye of the Kickstarter staff:

1. **Start with a strong idea—and express it clearly.** Choose a title which is short and clear. Don't overhype it. Proofread it to make sure your text is free of typos.

2. **Choose a compelling project image**. Make it clear, bright, and simple. Don't cover your images with badges ("Staff pick," "Free Shipping," "Live on Kickstarter," etc.), or other distracting graphics.

3. **Put the most important information first.** Make sure your project description page starts with a short and clear statement about what you're doing. Imagine that someone is skimming just the first two paragraphs. What information would you want them to see?

4. **Illustrate your description and rewards.** Do not limit yourself to text; use high-quality photos, videos, and GIFs in your description. Eye-catching images and GIFs make your story more engaging. Show something related to your creative process: your manuscript, illustrations, and moments from your writing life. Add images of your rewards in the project description.

5. **Stay oriented to your target audience and don't spam.** Send emails to those who have expressed their interest in receiving notifications from you. Don't promote your project where it shouldn't be promoted or send unsolicited messages to people you don't know. Whether you're doing it via email or on social networks, it's against Kickstarter's Community Guidelines and could get you suspended from the platform.

6. **Check other "Projects We Love" and subscribe to the Kickstarter newsletter.** This will help you to get an idea of which projects they feature. Most of them will have well-crafted videos, striking images, a clear plan, an excited community, and a lot of creativity. Maybe you will find some inspiration that you can use for your project.

As you can see, those tips aren't anything extraordinary. They just remind you that you actually need to focus on creating an authentic, purpose-driven campaign. Don't expect to be featured—or as has been said: hope for the best but plan for the worst.

Finally, you can write a short story about your project and send an email to stories@kickstarter.com. It is best to not send this immediately after launching your project, but after a more significant event, such as when your project is noticed by a famous media outlet, your video becomes viral, or you are interviewed about your project on some TV show. If you haven't reached any significant event, just write a short but heartfelt email, emphasizing why your project is important and exceptional. Since those emails are reviewed by Kickstarter staff, honesty and real emotions can influence their decisions.

If you are selected as "Projects We Love," what effect will it have on your campaign? I've discussed this question with many creators who were able to get the "Projects We Love" badge. Most of them were a bit disappointed with the results. They received a bit more traffic, but it didn't have any significant impact on funding. Some creators said it didn't bring any new backers and some told me this "might have brought" a few. So it seems that earning this badge doesn't really make a big difference.

Kickstarter's Social Networks

Kickstarter features some of the "Projects We Love" on social networks: Facebook, Twitter, and Instagram. I compared the results of the most recent projects that were mentioned on social networks and found that the highest engagement is achieved on Instagram.

Even though Kickstarter has over a million followers on Twitter and 1.5 million followers on Facebook, the post performance is really low. As I'm writing this text, I went to Kickstarter's Facebook page and checked the most recent book project they've shared. It was a children's book about the extraordinary achievements of Pakistani women. This post received twenty likes, one comment and four shares.

Then I went to Kicktraq, which shows daily pledges of Kickstarter projects, and checked what impact this had on the number of backers for this campaign. A day before the Facebook post there were four backers. On the same day of the Facebook post there were three backers and the next day, another three. It seems that this didn't have any impact at all. Try to do the same research by yourself and analyze the results. I'm sure you will come to a similar conclusion.

Instagram, on the other hand, has the highest post engagement, but it doesn't allow adding clickable links to images. Followers that want to learn more must go to Kickstarter's bio and find the link of an appropriate image there. As a result, none of the social media channels generate many visits for "Projects We Love."

Kickstarter's Newsletter

Kickstarter's mailing list has a large group of highly targeted potential backers who may be interested in funding worthy campaigns, even though they have no prior connection to the project. If you get featured in the platform's newsletter, you will certainly feel a much higher boost of traffic compared with sharing your project on Kickstarter's social media.

I am a subscriber of the "Projects We Love" newsletter and while I was writing this paragraph, I opened the most recent email, reviewed the featured projects, and checked their funding statistics in Kicktraq. All of them had a spike on that day. However, there's one problem. There are around 3,500 live campaigns on Kickstarter, and on average, four projects are featured in a weekly "Projects We Love" newsletter. So the chances of being selected are very low.

Popularity Algorithm

If you choose "Trending" projects on Kickstarter, they are sorted by "Popularity," which is an algorithm that creators try to hack. Kickstarter does not reveal this algorithm and its dynamics (how often it refreshes in the search) for obvious reasons. However, there are a few known factors that influence the rankings of specific projects:

- An investigation performed by Prefundia (you can find a detailed article here: http://prefundia.com/blog/hacking-kickstarters-popular-algorithm-how-to-become-most-popular) shows that the most heavily weighted metric within this algorithm is the number of backers per day. Suppose there are two identical projects and the first one has ten backers who pledged $100 each (total amount 10*100 = $1,000) and the other project has received one pledge of $1,000. The first one will get a higher "Popularity" ranking because even though the raised amount was the same, it attracted more backers in the same period. According to Prefundia, the percent funded and the total amount raised are the next drivers, though their impact is significantly less weighty.

- Another metric that may influence the "Popularity" algorithm is traffic volume to a project page within a certain time and traffic conversion rate (the better it converts, the higher the project appears in the Kickstarter search). Even though I cannot guarantee this is true, it does make sense—Kickstarter earns commissions from all successful projects, so it's in their interest to attract new visitors and get the best possible conversion rate.

So what conclusions can be made here? Nothing new—just follow all suggestions in the previous chapters: prepare a mailing list of your potential backers, establish relations with influencers, and perform other actions that may bring people to your campaign. Now you know that every backer counts, so don't forget to encourage your friends and family to support your project with at least a $1 pledge on day one. Everything else will be out of your control. If you appear higher in your category—great. If not—there's no need to worry.

What Happens If You Appear Higher in Your Category?

We've already discussed that even if you are selected for the "Projects We Love," this fact itself doesn't give you extra traffic. You should either be mentioned in the Kickstarter's newsletter, social networks, or appear higher in the platform's search.

If you appear on Kickstarter's newsletter, you will certainly get an increase of backers, but just for that one day. If you are mentioned on the platform's social channels, there's a chance that you will get some additional traffic, but it will be much lower than from the newsletter. Finally, if you appear higher in your category, the traffic you get will depend on your position and how long you can maintain it. Being in the top position can bring the most benefit for your campaign, but it's also the most difficult to achieve. All the creators I interviewed who managed to appear in the Top 20 in their category received extra backers from Kickstarter.

The Final Days of Your Project

The last days of your project are the last chance to get those backers who were interested, but delayed their decision for different reasons. It's very important that your project is fully funded by that time because seeing "100% funded" and a number of backers who have already provided their support makes it more compelling for others to back your project.

When someone browses Kickstarter and checks various projects, it's possible to click on a "Remind me" icon (see screenshot below of how it is displayed on Kickstarter) and be reminded about the project before it ends.

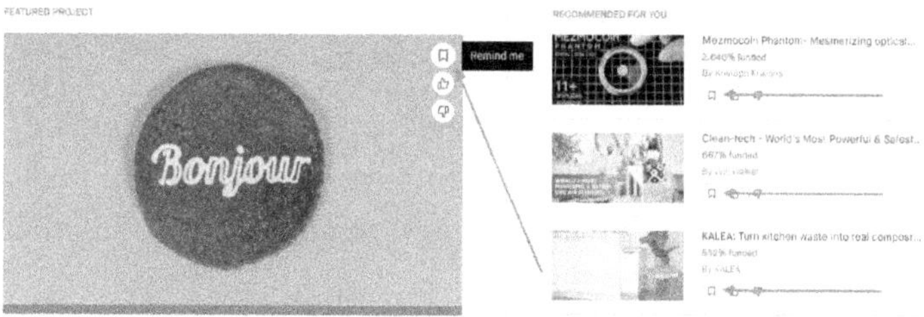

Forty-eight hours before the end of the campaign, Kickstarter automatically sends an email to those who pressed the "Remind me" button, but haven't backed the project yet. Visitors who clicked the "Remind me" button are called Followers. When you open the creator's dashboard, you can see how many Followers you have, how many have become your backers and what the conversion rate is (see screenshot below).

Project Followers

118   **19**   **16%**

Project Followers   Converted Followers   Conversion Rate

You cannot see who your Followers are, and some of them may be duplicated with contacts from your mailing list. Kickstarter sends a reminder for Followers forty-eight hours before the project ends, so my suggestion is to send one follow-up email to your mailing list before the Kickstarter reminder and one after. For example, sixty hours and twenty-four hours before the end of your campaign. You can also add a countdown timer (if your newsletter program supports this feature) in your email, which will create additional urgency.

You can also schedule posts on social media in advance (when sixty, forty-eight, twenty-four, twelve, six, and two hours are left). You may use Canva to easily create attractive and appropriately sized images for such posts.

Before your project ends, make your last project update. Express your gratitude for all who have shared and backed your project and make this final request to support your campaign.

What If Funding Is Unsuccessful?

A crowdfunding campaign is a small but important step in your book launch process. If you succeed in reaching your goal, congratulations! Say thank you to everyone who helped and contributed to your project, share your excitement with others, and take a moment to celebrate! Then get ready, because this is where the difficult phase starts—delivering what you have promised.

If funding was unsuccessful, do not worry. Failure is the teacher in your path to success. Try to understand the reasons behind this. Take your time to think this through and write down your conclusions. It's not always easy to understand the core reason for the failure, but it's worth writing your thoughts immediately, whether they are correct or not. We tend to forget things as time goes by, so having notes about our failures and successes makes it easy to access information from which we can learn something.

If your project was fine, but the campaign was unsuccessful, possible failure reasons could be related to:

- **Your project goal.** Maybe your project goal was too big? Then you can consider re-launching your campaign with a lower goal.

- **Your audience.** Maybe you didn't collect enough leads during pre-launch, or leads that you attracted didn't match the profile of your ideal customer?

- **Your marketing plan.** Did your advertising pay back? Maybe you weren't able to attract any backers from the platform because your book was too niche?

Once you've made necessary improvements, you can always re-launch your project. One last thing: unsuccessful projects are still accessible through Kickstarter's search, but the platform de-indexes them so they don't show up in external search engines.

Receiving the Funds

As mentioned before, when the backer chooses a reward and enters their credit card details, the platform only stores this information, but does not withdraw the money. Kickstarter starts charging credit cards only if the goal is reached and after the campaign has ended.

For various reasons, some of the credit cards may not be processed and you may lose some pledges. If a payment cannot be collected, the platform sends emails to such backers with instructions to fix their pledge and follows up with periodic reminders every forty-eight hours throughout the following week.

You can also go to your "Backer Report," sort it by "Errored pledges" and message those backers if you'd like to be involved in this process too. Backers will have seven days from the end of the project to fix their payments. After the end of this period, Kickstarter will try again to collect pledges, but if this second attempt also fails, such pledges will be dropped.

The pledge collection process takes fourteen days and then Kickstarter sends a report, which gives detailed information about gross and dropped pledges, refunds, the platform fee, payment processing fee, and final payment amount. The payout will be transferred to the bank account which you provided during project registration. Depending on the intermediary banks involved in the transfer process, you may need to wait for an additional three to fourteen business days for the funds to reach your account.

The last project I collaborated in received $16,864 gross pledges and of these $2,930 were dropped… That was more than 17% of the total funding! I was expecting that we might lose up to 10% due to different problems related to credit card processing, but 17% of dropped pledges really shocked me. Anyway, you can't predict everything. From the remaining amount of $13,934, Kickstarter deducted a 5% platform fee ($696.7) and around 3% ($430.87) for the payment processing, which left us with $12,806.43.

Don't forget taxes. In most cases, funds raised on Kickstarter are considered income. It is taxed differently depending on where you live. I recommend consulting with a local tax advisor and finding out what taxes you will have to pay.

Survey and Communication with Your Backers

Once you know the final list of backers whose payments went through, you can start creating a survey to collect shipping addresses and other necessary information related to your rewards.

You can send a survey through Kickstarter only once, so think through all the questions in advance. As fulfillment takes time, you may allow backers to change their shipping addresses until you're ready to actually ship rewards. Once you're ready to ship, you will need to indicate this on Kickstarter and backers will receive a notification that they have forty-eight hours to enter their final addresses.

You should continue communication with your backers through updates, keeping them in the loop and informing them about the progress of your project. Since the Kickstarter community has many first-time creators, backers tend to be more tolerant when it comes to late deliveries. But if you realize that you will not be able to keep to your promises to deliver by the estimated date, notify your backers as soon as possible. Post the project update and explain the situation. Be honest and open, because these people have contributed to the implementation of your idea.

Kickstarter "Spotlight" Feature

After successfully funding your project, you will have the opportunity to use the Kickstarter "Spotlight" feature, which allows you to customize your project page. You will be able to edit your description, title, and blurb, change the background (add a color or upload an image), upload a new project image, customize the button, and later point all page visitors to your landing page or a book page on Amazon.

TURN YOUR MANUSCRIPT INTO A BOOK

Crowdfunding helps you to verify whether there's a demand for your book, and if your campaign is successful, you will get money for self-publishing your book. If you started your crowdfunding campaign by having just a manuscript, you will have to turn it into a professional-looking book. To do that you will need to do the following:

- Ask if your readers are willing to read your manuscript and give their feedback.

- Collect their feedback and use it improve your manuscript.

- Edit your book.

- Create a cover design.

- Format your book.

- Print the first batch of your books and ship them to your backers.

- Upload your book to Amazon and other distribution channels.

Collect Feedback from Beta Readers

Beta readers are early readers of your manuscript who give feedback from the point of view of an average reader. You may invite people from your mailing list to become your beta readers or announce that you are looking for beta readers on your social media profile or on special reading/writing groups.

When I was writing this book, I announced that I was looking for beta readers on a few Facebook and Reddit groups related to writing. Here's the copy of my post in the Facebook group "The Write Life Community:"

> *Looking for beta readers for my new book. The book explains how to raise money for self-publishing your first book by using crowdfunding (Kickstarter). It's dedicated to first-time authors and for those who have already launched a book but struggle with sales. The story behind this book is based on my personal experience. I launched my first book 4 years ago and till now made around $18k income from it. The biggest part of the income was raised during the crowdfunding campaign and the rest were book sales on Amazon. Are there authors who would like to review my manuscript? If so, please write "Interested" and I'll contact you privately. If you have any questions, feel free to ask!*

Overall forty people expressed their interest to become beta readers and ten of them provided extensive feedback that I used to improve my manuscript. Special thanks to all of my beta readers! Even though beta reading prolongs the publishing process, I think it is a very valuable stage if you want to increase the quality of your book.

Some people may want to be your beta readers just because they are fans of your work. But if you are a first-time writer, you can attract beta readers by promising to give the final version of your book in return for their feedback. I used this method with my first and second books and it worked really well.

Finally, if your budget allows, you can hire beta readers. When I was searching for beta readers, I received an offer from a person who is labeled a Goodreads Top Reviewer (#7 in popularity and #23 most followed). She explained that due to the time and level of detail that she puts into each manuscript, she only offers paid beta reading. Her minimal rate was $15 for 10,000 words, then $1 for every additional thousand words with a turnaround time of two weeks or less.

How to Hire Professionals for Publishing Work

My recommendation is to hire professionals and delegate editing, cover/interior design and formatting to them, unless you are very skilled in one of those areas and insist on doing this yourself. I mainly use Fiverr and sometimes Upwork to find freelancers for publishing work. Most people evaluate Fiverr freelancers by reviews, but there's also another great way to choose the right freelancer that worked very well for me. I'll explain it in more detail.

On Fiverr, most freelancers offer a small gig for $5. For one of my books I needed translation services. I picked a few freelancers who had positive reviews and contacted them privately, asking if they could translate a sample text for $5. I then selected three freelancers who agreed to do this and I made the orders. In two days, I received the translated files and sent them to my editor. I asked him to edit those translations and to evaluate which of the translations was done the best, in his opinion. Overall, I spent $25 on this experiment and it helped me to choose the best freelancer for translation services.

You can use the same method if you want to get some validation of freelancers' work before you hire them. For example, if you want to hire an editor, ask if they can edit your sample text for $5. Order this gig from three editors, compare their final work, and make a decision about which one is the best fit for you.

It makes sense to apply this process only if you order more expensive services. However, you don't need to do that for small tasks because following this process takes a bit more time and requires you to spend some money on samples.

Choosing an Editor

When I hired an editor for my first book, I didn't use the method that I have just described, and as a result, I ended up with an editor who wasn't a good fit for me. I trust she did her job well, but it seems that we had some communication issues because she kept asking how I preferred one or another word to be written and I thought that she should have been determining this. Moreover, when she sent the edited manuscript, I was not able to see her changes because "Track Changes" wasn't turned on when she was editing my file. Luckily, we agreed to finish our cooperation in a way that satisfied both parties.

After this experience, I became more careful in selecting who to hire, and the method that I described (ordering a sample gig from a few freelancers) helped me to choose the right editor. Interestingly, he edited my manuscript several times faster and at half the rate of my first editor. It seems that the price does not always determine the quality of work.

How much does the editing cost? It depends on the type of editing you need. These are a few different types of book editing, listed from the most expensive to the least expensive:

- **Developmental editing.** An in-depth edit of your manuscript. You will get a full, substantial, and structural edit. A developmental edit will come early in the publication process, while you are still in the drafting stage. Rewrites happen in this editing phase.

- **Copy editing.** Your editor checks for grammar, spelling, punctuation, syntax, sentence structure, and consistency issues.

- **Proofreading.** The last step in the editing process, when your editor checks the proof against typesetting specifications and other inconsistencies.

Most first-time self-published authors (including me) cannot afford developmental editing, so they usually hire editors to do the copy editing and proofreading. The editor that I use for copy editing charges me $5 per 1,000 words and I am quite satisfied with his rate and his quality of work.

Creating a Cover Design

While your editor is working on your manuscript, you can find a graphic designer who will create a professional book cover that is appealing for your target audience. My first choice to find a graphic designer for this work was 99designs. It is a global creative platform for custom graphic design, where you can hire a talented designer by launching a design contest.

I chose the minimal plan—the "Bronze package" that costs $299, and guarantees at least thirty design concepts. I created a brief for the book cover and launched the public design contest. Then I did one trick that helped me to get many more design concepts than 99designs promised in their plan. I decided to actively invite freelancers to participate in my contest by writing them personal messages. As a result, I received almost 100 cover design samples! That's a lot to choose from! Of course, most of them were horrible and out of 100, I selected just ten. I told designers what else to improve and selected the top three. Then I asked my Kickstarter backers to express their vote and based on the results, selected the winner.

If you can afford paying $299 for your book cover, you should definitely try 99designs, but if you want to get this job done at a lower rate, there's an alternative—finding a graphic designer on Fiverr. There are freelancers on Fiverr who propose creating a book cover for as low as $5. But realistically if you care about the quality, you will spend more. For example, I paid $52.50 for the cover design (see below) of my book *Your First Kickstarter Campaign*.

I also used some graphs and diagrams in the book and paid $83.75 for the graphic designer on Fiverr to create twenty hand-drawn illustrations. One of the illustrations was used as the main image for my book cover.

Formatting Your Book

The final step to turning your manuscript into a book is formatting. As you may have already gathered, my suggestion is to hire someone who can handle the formatting process for you. The cost of your book's interior formatting will vary, depending on the length of your book, how many images, graphs, tables, and other specific features your book has, whether you need an ebook or print formatting, and the type of your book distribution channels. For example, if you plan to upload your book to Amazon, there are many freelancers who do this type of formatting, so it will not cost you much (I will share how much I paid for this service), but if you want to print the book at some local printing house with specific requirements, it may cost you much more (I ended up paying a few times more than for the standard Amazon formatting, more on this later).

My first book contained around 56,000 words, fifteen images and a few tables. I paid $94.50 for the formatting of the paperback version, and then additional $63 for the ebook formatting. The second book contained a similar number of words, but three times more images. This time I chose another freelancer and spent even less—$78 for both ebook and paperback formatting. So realistically you can expect to spend between $100–$150 for the book formatting. There are many freelancers on Fiverr who can assist you with this task.

You can find suitable freelancers on Fiverr by typing one of the following keywords: "book layout design" (sometimes called "typesetting" or "interior design"), "interior book design," or "book formatting." You'll notice that some freelancers specialize in formatting books to meet the requirements of specific platforms. In such a case they include this information in the description of their service, for example, "I will format your book for Kindle KDP, IngramSpark, Lulu, Barnes & Noble, etc."

I've already mentioned that if you want your books to be available on Amazon, you'll have to create an account on KDP. So your priority is to choose a freelancer who will format your manuscript and will create an ebook and paperback according to the KDP requirements. Later, if you want to add more distribution channels (I recommend Draft2Digital and IngramSpark), you may order formatting of your book for other platforms. Most ebook distribution platforms use the EPUB file format, so converting your manuscript into two digital formats: MOBI (KDP format) and EPUB will be enough.

Here's a list of items that proper formatting usually includes:

- **Professional book layout design.** You may find some samples in a freelancer's portfolio, but if they don't display this information, contact them privately and ask to send some samples of their work. Choose only those freelancers who have layouts with a professional look and feel. Another method is to find the layout design that you like by doing some search on Google Images or Pinterest. Then share your favorite layout design with a freelancer and ask if they have done something similar. If they respond positively, ask them to send the most similar example from their portfolio.

- **Table of contents.** If formatting is done for the ebook, a table of contents should be clickable.

- **Adding page numbering, and running header and footer (sometimes called running head and foot).** The running header is at the top of the page and the running footer is at the bottom. They can contain the title of the book, page numbers, a part of a book, a chapter, or any other reference point. They are on most, but not all pages. For example, there is no need to add numbers and running header and footer to blank pages.

- **Paragraphs formatting.** This includes paragraph indentation, adding proper margins and line spacing. You may consider using *drop caps*. A drop cap is a large capital letter, much bigger in size than the rest of the letters that follow. It is used as a decorative element at the beginning of a paragraph or chapter.

- **Formatting chapters.** Chapters should start on the right page.

- **Copyright page.** Even though it is optional, the copyright statement protects your work. It includes the following information about a book: the author's name, the publisher's name (if you self-publish the book as an organization), the year the book was published, legal disclaimers, and its ISBN (the International Standard Book Number). An ISBN isn't required for ebooks, but every printed book needs it. You can receive a free ISBN from your self-publishing platform, such as KDP, Lulu, Draft2Digital, or IngramSpark, or you can purchase an ISBN from your regionally accepted source.

- **Clickable links, footnotes, endnotes.** This is applied only for ebook formatting. Readers should be able to click on links, footnotes, and endnotes.

Also, pay attention to the number of formatting revisions, available in the order. Some freelancers charge for additional revisions and some include unlimited formatting revisions in their offer. Once your manuscript is properly formatted, it will be ready to upload to KDP. After creating an account on KDP, you will be able to evaluate the formatting of your ebook by using Kindle Previewer and order a proof copy of your paperback.

Printing Your Book

Major book distribution platforms, such as KDP and IngramSpark, that provide services for self-published authors can print your book on demand and subtract your printing costs from your royalties. Print on demand is a great service because you don't have to pay any costs upfront or carry any inventory. Moreover, you can order proofs and author copies of your paperbacks.

After successfully completing the crowdfunding campaign for my first book, I continued pre-orders by reaching out to my business contacts directly. To meet this demand, I needed to print 300 books and send them to my readers from thirty-five different countries. So I started to look for the most cost-effective way to print and ship these books.

I found out that there's digital and offset printing. I won't go into technical details about the differences of these technologies, but the general rule is this. Digital printing is cheaper if you want to print a small quantity of books. Offset printing is more economical if you print at least 500-1,000 books. There's usually a minimum quantity requirement for offset printing and a greater volume lowers your price significantly.

It was clear that in my case I should choose digital printing, so I started sending requests to different printing houses and book distribution platforms that allow ordering author copies. After comparing the quotes, I chose IngramSpark, which belongs to the Ingram Content Group that also manages Lightning Source. Lightning Source is oriented to mid to large size publishers, and IngramSpark serves the needs of independent publishers.

However, prices change as time goes by. While writing this text, I checked how much it would cost me now to print 300 copies of my book *Your First Kickstarter Campaign,* which has the following specifications:

- Page count: 264

- Trim size: 5.5" x 8.5" (140mm x 216 mm)

- Interior color: black & white

- Paper: white

- Binding type: perfect bound

- Laminate type (KDP calls it "cover finish"): matte

These were the total costs that did not include shipping and applicable taxes: IngramSpark: $1,345.99 and KDP: $1,198.20. For accurate calculations, you would also need to add shipping fee and applicable taxes. If you are curious to estimate how much it would cost to print your books, you can use the following resources:

- The IngramSpark calculator is available online: https://myaccount.ingramspark.com/Portal/Tools/Shipping-Calculator

- The KDP calculator can be downloaded here: https://kdp.amazon.com/en_US/help/topic/G200735480#royalty_calculator

kindle direct publishing royalty calculator

Figures generated by this tool are for estimation purposes only. Your actual royalty will be calculated when you set up your book.

1. Enter interior type:	Black Ink
2. Enter number of pages:	264
3. Choose a distribution channel:	Amazon.com
4. Enter anticipated list price ($):	$19,99
Printing cost:	$4,02
Minimum list price:	$6,70
Amazon royalty:	$7,98
Expanded Distribution royalty:	$3,98

Printing costs on KDP depend only on page count and ink type (black or color). Trim size, bleed settings, and cover finish don't affect the printing cost. However, if you decide to choose some offset printing house, their pricing policy might be different. The costs may vary depending on paper thickness, page count, ink type (black ink or color ink), trim size, cover type (paperback or hardcover), cover finish (glossy or matte), etc. If you are not familiar with some of these common book printing terms, you can do some research on Google and read relevant groups and forums.

I've mentioned that offset printing is more economical if you print at least 500-1,000 books. If your order is within this range or higher, do some research and create a list of potential printing houses. Don't limit yourself by looking for suppliers in your area—you will be surprised that sometimes it's more economical to print books outside your country. Then create an email template that includes your requirements and reach out to those printing houses, asking them to send a quote for printing and shipping. Here's an example:

Hello,

I want to print 1,000 copies of my book. The requirements are:

** Trim size: 5.5" x 8.5"*

** Interior: one "color" (black)*

** Paper: 90 GSM white paper*

** Number of pages: 264*

** Cover finish: matte*

** Book binding: perfect bound*

Please send me your offer.

You can use an email automation tool such as Yet Another Mail Merge to reach out to a list of potential suppliers at once. After evaluating all the quotes, you can make a decision whether to choose KDP, IngramSpark, or a specific printing house. You should also take into account the printing house requirements for the book file. Requirements can be very specific and as a result, you will end up paying more for the book formatting services.

Before publishing *Your First Kickstarter Campaign* on Amazon, I released it in my home country—Lithuania—in Lithuanian, which is my native tongue. We don't have any print on demand companies here, so I had to print the books and send them to local distributors. I decided to print 2,000 copies and reached out to a few local printing companies. By choosing offset printing and ordering a greater volume, I was able to lower the price significantly. The total printing cost was $2,998. Just to compare, printing the same number of copies on KDP would cost me around $7,980. As you can see, the difference is significant.

However, the printing house had specific requirements for the book file, and I paid $320.25 for the book formatting according to their specifications. In comparison, formatting according to the KDP requirements was much cheaper—$78 for both ebook and paperback formatting. Another issue was storing the books at home. Here's the picture of what these 2,000 copies looked like:

While storing books at home may be a viable option if you print a few hundred books or you're lucky enough to have the available space, for most people, there just isn't enough room. Most likely I wouldn't print the same amount of books in the future due to the limited space at home. I would prefer to print 500 copies and then, if the sales go well, I would go with another 500 and so on. But in the most ideal scenario I wouldn't print books at all and would use only print on demand services. That's why I love dealing with KDP and IngramSpark, where someone else is responsible for book printing, storing, and shipping.

UPLOAD YOUR BOOK TO KDP

I assume that by now you have kept your promises to your backers and fulfilled your Kickstarter rewards. Your backers have already paid for your self-publishing work, so now you can reach new audiences and enjoy passive income from book sales on print on demand platforms and ebook stores.

When I started with my first book I used CreateSpace (now KDP Print) for paperback and KDP for the ebook. However, now you can publish both paperback and ebook through KDP, which makes it even easier to manage. In addition to KDP, you can consider using the following platforms: IngramSpark, Draft2Digital, or Smashwords. All of them are aggregators and can distribute your books to various sales channels. However, if we compare KDP to others, it is a clear winner as it has generated more than 80% of the passive income from book sales for me. So I will first cover how to upload your book to KDP and then we will review other possibilities.

Self-publishing your book on KDP is free. The first step is to sign up on their website https://kdp.amazon.com/. When you have your KDP account ready, you will need to upload a book cover and formatted manuscript that you have previously received from the freelancers that you hired for the book formatting job.

To make sure your ebook is formatted correctly, you should open it with Kindle Previewer, and for paperback you should order a proof copy. If you notice some errors, you can ask your freelancer to fix them and reupload corrected files once again until they look good.

If you are new to KDP, there's a great guide for newbies, named "KDP Jumpstart." You can check it out here: https://kdp.amazon.com/en_US/help/topic/G202187740. But in general, filling in all needed details, such as title, subtitle, author name, and book description is self-explanatory, so I will explain only those parts where you need to pay more attention.

Choosing Keywords and Categories

A lot of people forget that Amazon is a product-based search engine designed for making purchases. You must do proper keyword research and select the most relevant ones before you publish your book on KDP. The platform allows you to add up to seven search keywords that describe your book and place it into two categories. This will help your target readers find your book in searches on Amazon.

You can enter one or a few words in a keyword field. One-word keywords are often highly competitive, so it's better to choose long-tail keywords that are less competitive because they position your book in a specific niche. Your keywords should accurately reflect the words that potential readers will use when they search for a book on Amazon. Simply go to Amazon search, enter a keyword, and you will see that Amazon will suggest phrases that readers have used when looking to buy a book. Here's an example of long-tail keywords that Amazon suggests when I enter "self-publishing" to the Amazon search.

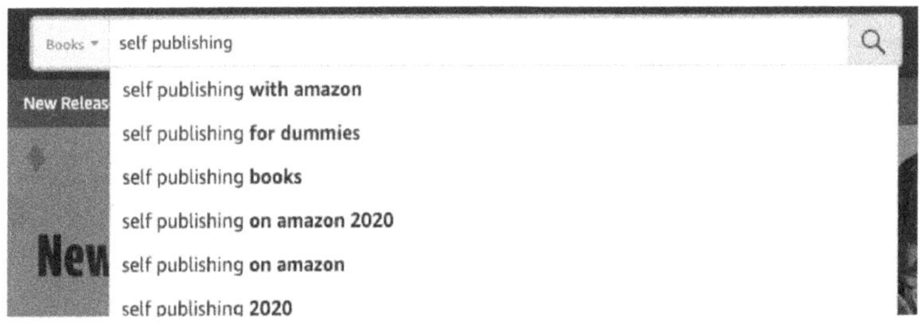

Along with factors like the Amazon Best Sellers Rank and book sales history, relevant keywords can boost your placement in search results on Amazon. So if you want to increase your chances of getting organic sales on Amazon, consider adding some specific keywords to your book title, subtitle, and description.

When you list your ebook on KDP, you get to choose only the two categories that are the most accurate based on the subject matter of your book. It's not so hard to choose them. Just browse the categories on the left under the Kindle Store > Kindle eBooks header and find books similar to yours. When you select a book, scroll down to "Product details" and next to the Amazon Best Sellers Rank, you will see a list of categories that this book is in. Here's an example of the "Product details" of my book *Your First Kickstarter Campaign*:

- **Item Weight :** 10.9 ounces

- **Paperback :** 262 pages

- **ISBN-10 :** 169008412X

- **ISBN-13 :** 978-1690084129

- **Publisher :** Independently published (September 25, 2019)

- **Product Dimensions :** 5.5 x 0.6 x 8.5 inches

- **Language :** English

- **Best Sellers Rank :** #439,721 in Books (See Top 100 in Books)

- #76 in Crowdfunding (Books)
- #84 in Product Management
- #510 in Marketing for Small Businesses (Books)

After analyzing a few similar books, you will be able to pick a relevant category easily. It's recommended you choose specific categories (instead of general ones) and "cross-categorize" by picking sub-categories in two different categories. For example, this book could be under "Writing Skills" in the category "Business & Money," and "Nonfiction" in another category "Writing, Research & Publishing Guides." Don't worry about picking the "perfect" keywords and categories. You will be able to change them later in your KDP dashboard if you want to experiment and try something new.

Finally, there's one tip that allows your book to have more than two categories. You can actually contact KDP support from your KDP dashboard and request your book to be placed in additional categories. Here's the message that I wrote:

Hello,

Please use the following categories for my book "Your First Kickstarter Campaign"

Amazon.com (Kindle)

Kindle Store > Kindle eBooks > Business & Money > Marketing & Sales > Advertising > Home-Based Business

Kindle Store > Kindle eBooks > Business & Money > Marketing & Sales > Advertising > Online Advertising

Kindle Store > Kindle eBooks > Business & Money > Investing > Crowdfunding

Amazon.com (Paperback)

Books > Business & Money > Finance > Crowdfunding

Books > Business & Money > Marketing & Sales > Marketing > Product Management

Books > Business & Money > Small Business & Entrepreneurship > Marketing

As you can see, I specified three categories (even though KDP allows you to select only two categories) for both Kindle and paperback. In addition to this, I listed other Amazon marketplaces (amazon.co.uk, amazon.de, amazon.ca, etc.) and wrote specific categories where I wanted my book to be listed. Amazon then reviewed my request, determined that my book was an appropriate fit for them, and listed the book in these categories.

Setting Your Pricing and Royalty

KDP offers two royalty options: 35% and 70%. You get 70% royalties (after delivery fees, which are based on your ebook file size) on ebooks that are priced between $2.99 and $9.99, and 35% royalties on any other price. (There are some exceptions to this rule if you enroll in KDP Select and create a Kindle Countdown Deal.) As you can see, $2.99–$9.99 is the sweet spot for authors because most buyers purchase books on Amazon within this price range. That's why the platform rewards those authors who stay in this range by giving them the highest royalty.

The paperback royalty rate is 60% for Amazon marketplaces and 40% if you enable "Expanded Distribution." Paperback royalties on KDP are calculated from the book's list price minus printing costs. You can calculate the printing costs and royalties by downloading the "Printing cost and royalty calculator" here: https://kdp.amazon.com/en_US/help/topic/G200735480#royalty_calculator. For example, your list price is $15. Your book is a 333-page paperback with black ink sold through:

- Amazon marketplaces, then your royalty is: (0.60 x $15) - $4.85 = $4.15;

- Expanded Distribution channels, then your royalty is: (0.40 x \$15) - \$4.85 = \$1.15.

If you don't want to keep all your eggs in one basket and earn slightly higher royalties, you can open an account with IngramSpark directly. In this case, you won't be able to choose the "Expanded Distribution" option on KDP. So, it's either KDP for standard distribution to Amazon marketplaces and IngramSpark for expanded distribution, or it's KDP all the way. I have an account on Ingram Spark, but sales from this platform are just 10% of what I've made on Amazon. However, I still plan to use IngramSpark and other platforms in the future because depending on one platform (Amazon) seems too risky to me.

Enroll in KDP Select

The KDP Select program allows you to spread the word about your book, reach more readers and earn more money. When you enroll in this program, you sign a 90-day agreement to sell your book exclusively on Amazon, and during this time, you are not allowed to publish your ebook on any other vendor site.

KDP Select puts your book in the Kindle Unlimited (KU) and the Kindle Owners' Lending Library (KOLL). Kindle Unlimited is a subscription service for Amazon users that costs \$9.99 per month and allows them to read as much as they want, choosing from over one million titles and thousands of audiobooks. Kindle Owners' Lending Library is available for Kindle owners with Amazon Prime memberships and it allows them to choose from thousands of books to read for free once a month. A good thing is that you get royalties even if someone from Kindle Unlimited and the Kindle Owners' Lending Library borrows and reads your book. You can even become a best-seller without selling a single book because borrowing also influences the Amazon best-seller rank.

There are two promotional tools offered by the KDP Select program:

- **Kindle Countdown Deal.** A time-bound promotion, where you can choose to discount your book as low as $0.99 (or do an incremental price increase) for up to seven days. You get to maintain the same 70% royalty (even if the price drops to less than $0.99). Pricing must remain unchanged for thirty days before and fourteen days after this program.

- **Free Book Promotion.** Readers can get your book for free up to five days. You can use this time to get more exposure and boost your ebook downloads.

You can run one of the above promos every ninety days, but they are the most valuable as a part of your book launch strategy.

BOOK LAUNCH AND MARKETING STRATEGY

Next, I will share my book launch and marketing strategy that I am constantly improving. This strategy wasn't invented by me. It consists of steps that I learned from people who are active in the self-publishing world: Tom Corson-Knowles, Stefan Pylarinos, Nick Stephenson, Chandler Bolt, Mark Dawson, and others. It's important to understand that what works for others doesn't always work for you. So be prepared to fail, learn from your mistakes, and figure out what gets you the best results.

Getting Reviews

Reviews are important for all books, especially if they are sold online. Would you buy a book without any reviews, written by an unknown author? I guess not. That's why your goal during the first launch week is to get at least a few positive reviews as soon as possible. Having at least a few reviews adds credibility for your book and then you can start actively promoting it. In addition to this, you must have a system that will help you get more reviews without having to spend too much time on this.

Customer reviews on Amazon are rated by a number of stars (1-5) and can have the "Verified Purchase" tag, which means that the reviewer bought the book on Amazon. If a review does not have this tag, it means that the reviewer didn't buy it on Amazon. Maybe such readers bought the book elsewhere, received it for free, borrowed it from the library, or used Kindle Unlimited (KU). Verified purchase reviews are given more weight by Amazon than non-tagged reviews.

When I self-published my first book, it was much easier to get reviews on Amazon than these days. Now, if someone wants to add a customer review, they must have spent at least $50 on Amazon using a valid credit or debit card in the past 12 months. This requirement can be considered a positive improvement for buyers because it has removed reviews by fake accounts and paid reviewers. On the other hand, it has created a new barrier for authors to collect reviews. So if some of your readers try to leave a review on Amazon and they get an error like this (see screenshot below), it means they are not eligible to do that.

> ! We apologize but this account has not met the minimum eligibility requirements to write a review. If you would like to learn more about our eligibility requirements, please see our community guidelines.

In addition to this, Amazon doesn't allow reviews written by your close friends or relatives, and you can't offer payment or any other incentive, such as gift certificates, bonus content, discounts on future purchases, or other gifts for someone to write a review. Is there a legitimate way to encourage leaving a review? Amazon allows offering *free advance copies* of your book—just that it must be clear that you welcome all feedback, both positive and negative. Here's their quote:

> *You may provide free or discounted copies of your books to readers. However, you may not demand a review in exchange or attempt to*

influence the review. Offering anything other than a free or discounted copy of the book—including gift cards—will invalidate a review, and we'll have to remove it.

Giving Advance Reading Copies of Your Book

An *advance reading copy* (ARC) or advance copy is a free copy of a new book given to target readers before the book is published. These readers in the self-publishing world are often referred to as a *launch team*. They help you to launch your book by reading it in advance and leaving a review after the book is live.

Giving advance reading copies is a common practice in publishing and this ensures that authors get some reviews when the book is launched. As long as you make it clear that you welcome both positive and negative feedback, you can do this and it's not against Amazon policy. But you can't solicit people to review your book.

How do you form your own launch team? Leverage your existing contacts and invite them to help you. Reach out to your followers on social networks, readers of your blog, subscribers of your newsletter, backers of your Kickstarter campaign, members of the same community, or your friends who want to support you.

Before launching the book *Your First Kickstarter Campaign* on Amazon, I gathered a mailing list of around 400 people who were interested in a crowdfunding topic. Here's the screenshot of the email that I sent to them:

Hi ,

Happy to announce that the book "Your First Kickstarter Campaign" will be officially launched on Amazon this month!

Thanks for staying with me this far!

Now I'm building a launch team of people who would like to support my book by reading it in advance and leaving an honest review on Amazon once the book is launched.

Members of the launch team will get a free PDF copy of the ebook.

Would you like to join the launch team?

To join click on "YES" and I'll send you a free ebook and further instructions.

Those who clicked on "Yes" received another email automatically:

Hi,

Welcome to the launch team of the book "Your First Kickstarter Campaign."

I'm glad you've decided to support the launch of this book!

As promised, here's your free ebook:

>> Download the ebook here <<

The book will be launched on Amazon on 24th September, so I'd appreciate it if you could read the book before then.

Once the book is launched, I will notify you by email and will explain how you can leave an honest review on Amazon.

That's it for now. If you have any questions, let me know.

Glad to have you here!

When the book was launched on Amazon, I emailed my launch team again. However, now I would do certain things differently. I wasn't aware of the new Amazon customer review eligibility requirements. There were many people in my launch team who hadn't spent $50 on Amazon in the past twelve months. As a result, they couldn't leave a review even if they wanted to. Now, I'd sort this out in advance by asking the launch team members if they met the Amazon eligibility requirements. If they didn't, I would ask them to leave a review on another platform, such as GoodReads, that doesn't have such strict requirements.

It's important to mention that if someone from your launch team leaves a review, it's better to do that two to three days after reading the book. Even if they read the book before then, it is still better to go to the end of the book after downloading it. An instant review may seem suspicious because it's unrealistic that someone would read a book and decide to leave feedback so quickly. Amazon fights with review solicitation and fake reviews and as a result, suspicious reviews can be removed.

When someone leaves a review, it may become public within 72 hours after being submitted. Sometimes it can take even longer because Amazon uses different algorithms to filter faulty reviews. So, realistically, you can expect the first reviews to appear by the end of the first week after the book's launch day.

You need to create ideal conditions for your launch team to leave a review. Even if someone downloads your book for free during your Free Book Promotion (you can run it if you enrolled your book in the KDP Select program), Amazon still considers it a zero dollar purchase. It means that if such reviews are not filtered by Amazon, they will be marked as "Verified Purchase." Only "borrows" by KU readers will not show up as "Verified Purchases." Running a free book promotion is the easiest way to encourage your launch team to download your book. If for some reason you don't want to make your book temporarily free, selling your book for $0.99 is your second best bet to maximize the number of people getting your book.

Include a Review Request at the End of the Book

In general, readers are not really thinking about leaving a review, even if they have truly enjoyed reading a book. That's why it's a good practice to include a review request at the end of the book. It's easy to add this text to your manuscript and doesn't require any further action from you. If you do this, the rule of thumb is one review for every 100 sales or every 1,000 freebies if you enroll your book in KDP Select and run a free book promotion. Just say "thanks" for reading your book and ask them politely to leave an honest review. Here's the review request that I use in my book:

> *I hope you enjoyed this book! It would be greatly appreciated if you left an honest review on Amazon. As you know, reader reviews are very useful in making choices whether to read a book or not, so I invite you to add your voice to the mix.*
>
> *Thanks so much!*

Previously I covered how to use a reader magnet in your book to encourage readers to sign up to your mailing list. In this case, when you create an email sequence for your readers, add a review request to one of your emails. This is a one-time job that will help you get more reviews as more people buy your book.

Encourage Reviews If You Are Approached by a Reader

Getting reviews is a continuous process, so develop a habit of asking for a review whenever you are approached by someone who purchased and read your book. If you get a message from a reader who has just read your book, ask if they enjoyed it.

Most readers respond positively, and in this case, ask if they could leave an honest review. Don't forget to explain how important the reviews are for your book. I've personally developed this habit, and in my case it works even better than a review request in the book. From time to time, I get messages from readers saying that they enjoyed my book, and I always ask them to leave an honest review.

Author Central Account and Editorial Reviews

There are two types of reviews on Amazon: customer reviews that are written by regular readers who bought the book on Amazon (we've already covered them) and editorial reviews that can be added by the author via the Author Central Account.

Even though Amazon suggests that Editorial Reviews should be obtained from reputable and relevant publications, including the *New York Times Book Review* and *Publisher's Weekly*, the truth is that you can post any reviews there. For example, I posted reviews that I received from my beta readers, but you can even post feedback that you received from your friends who read your book.

Creating an Author Central Account is possible only when your book is live, and having it allows you to:

- add your biography, photos, videos, blog and editorial reviews;
- see the list of your books and your author rank;
- track your book sales and check their sales rank over time;
- check your customer reviews.

Collecting Reviews During the First Launch Week

When you launch your book on Amazon, you must have social proof that the book you introduce is really good. It may take up to one week for the first reviews to appear with the help of your launch team. That's why your main goal during the first launch week is to collect at least a few positive reviews. Only then you can start active promotion of your book.

When you are ready to publish your book, click on "Save and Publish" to submit your book. English titles are typically reviewed and published within twelve hours, while non-English titles take around forty-eight hours to review and publish. Send an email with a link to your book to your launch team as soon as the book is live. Download your book ebook and order a proof copy of your paperback to double-check there are no errors.

You can either run the Free Book Promotion for one to two days, so that your launch team can download your book, or you can launch it for $0.99 if for some reason you don't want to make your book temporarily free. When you create an email for your launch team, you may remind them that even if they have already read your manuscript, they should download/purchase the book on Amazon (else their review won't be marked as "Verified Purchase") and scroll to the end of the book (else Amazon might think that this is a faulty review, and it can be filtered).

Send a follow-up email after a few days and thank everyone for leaving their honest reviews, even if they haven't done this yet. A gentle reminder will encourage some of those who have procrastinated leaving a review to now. You may also send a third email after a week, and share a few reviews that you received from your closest fans—this could be your last mass email related to reviews.

Earn a New Release or Best Seller Badge

Another goal of the book launch strategy is to earn a New Release or Best Seller badge. This is a sort of social proof, similar to reviews, and it amplifies the promotional efforts for your book and helps reach new readers.

To be eligible for the New Release badge, your book has to be one of the top three best-selling books by sales rank in your category and it should have been published within the last thirty days. That's why the first month is a great opportunity for your book to get additional exposure by Amazon.

Here you can see an example, where my book was #1 New Release in the "Startups" category. It had several positive reviews—not a lot, but enough at that stage. Positive reviews together with a New Release badge provide social proof that the book is valuable, and is worth purchasing.

Your First Kickstarter Campaign: Step by Step Guide to Launching a Successful Crowdfunding Project Kindle Edition

by Vilius Stanislovaitis (Author)

4 ratings

#1 New Release in Startups

See all 2 formats and editions

Kindle	Paperback
$1.20	$14.99
Read with Our Free App	2 New from $14.99

63% of Kickstarter campaigns fail. Do this one thing, and you'll be among the 37% who succeed.

How can you earn the Best Seller badge? You need to outsell the best-selling book in your category. When you choose categories for your book, you should carefully evaluate the competition. Find a relevant niche category, where the best-selling book doesn't have a high Amazon Best Sellers Rank. Placing your book in such a category will require a smaller average number of sales than the large category. This will increase your chances of getting a Best Seller badge. For example, I chose the category "Telephone Systems Engineering" for my first book, so it wasn't that hard to become the #1 Best Seller.

Books › Engineering & Transportation › Engineering

Look inside ↓

How to Start a VoIP Business: A Six-Stage Guide to Becoming a VoIP Service Provider Paperback – February 15, 2016

by Vilius Stanislovaitis ˅ (Author)

☆ ☆ ☆ ☆ ☆ ˅   45 customer reviews

#1 Best Seller in Telephone Systems Engineering

› See all 3 formats and editions

Kindle	Paperback
$12.09	$24.99

Read with Our **Free App**   15 Used from $27.78
14 New from $24.99

Is It Worth Using Free Book Promotion?

Using Free Book Promotion is optional, and you may decide on your own whether to use it or not. When I ran this promotion, it didn't bring the results that I had expected, but I know that other authors were able to use it quite well.

What is the goal in giving your book away free of charge? This can be your marketing strategy that works particularly well if you have a book series (or few other books within the same niche that are closely linked) and make the first book in a series free. Having a free book allows you to increase its downloads significantly. If you use a reader magnet inside your book, you can expect that a part of those who download your book will sign up on your landing page. This helps you to grow your audience, and later you can promote other relevant books to your subscribers.

However, if you have just one book and there's nothing else that you can sell, making your book free has fewer benefits. You can expect to get a few additional leads by putting a reader magnet inside your book, and make a few extra sales immediately after the transition of the book from free to paid. I'll explain how that works.

After launching the free promotion, you should follow your book's ranking, and when you see that it no longer increases, you should cut your promotion manually and transition your book from free to $0.99. Even if you manually end your promotion, your book will still remain highly ranked in the free book category for one to two hours. The idea of this transition is to use this time period and aim for some of the people who see your book in the free category to not mind buying it for $0.99. These sales will increase your rankings in the paid category.

As you have already read, I combined a Free Book Promotion with additional advertising on book promotion sites for my book *Your First Kickstarter Campaign*. It was downloaded 1,127 times within twenty-four hours. Such number of downloads pushed the book and it was ranked as the 115th free ebook in the Kindle Store and appeared in the first place in all relevant categories: "Business & Investing," "Startups," and "Crowdfunding." Then I transitioned my book from free to paid. Even though it was emotionally rewarding seeing my book so high on Amazon rankings, it didn't help to grow my audience—only three people signed up on my landing page. Moreover, there were just two sales, after my book became paid again.

So even though there are many self-publishers who recommend this strategy, my suggestion is not to expect too much from it. My personal experience was negative because the money I invested didn't pay back. Next, I will share how much I spend on book promotion sites and what the outcome was.

Book Promotion Sites

Your goal during the period when your book is free or highly discounted is to raise your Amazon Best Sellers Rank as high as possible, by combining free promotion with other marketing initiatives. One such initiative is submitting your book to promotion sites that list books that are either deeply discounted or free. These sites then send newsletters to their subscribers who want to be informed about highly discounted or free books in particular categories.

However, out of a few hundred sites, just a few are worth your attention. Dave Chesson, better known as Dave the Kindlepreneur, lists over 127 book promotion sites on his blog https://kindlepreneur.com/list-sites-promote-free-amazon-books/, but when I reached out to him personally he recommended just a few:

- Awesome Gang,
- BKnights (available on Fiverr),
- Book Sends,
- Ereader News Today (ENT),
- Free Kindle Books and Tips (FKBT),
- Freebooksy,
- The Fussy Librarian,
- Robin Reads.

In addition to this, Dave recommends adding Amazon Ads and BookBub to the combo, but we'll talk about these options later. I've tried all of the above sites except Awesome Gang, ENT, and FKBT and I will share my results with you.

Keep in mind that some of the book promotion sites have some minimum book requirements. For example, Freebooksy requires a minimum of 50,000 words; Book Sends requires at least five reviews, with a high overall average, an attractive cover, and a planned sale price of less than $3 and at least 50% off full price.

I launched my book for $0.99 and at first it was promoted by Robin Reads for $60, and I sold seventeen books on that day. The next day, I used BKnights promotion for $5, and sold five books. On the third day my book was promoted by The Fussy Librarian for $23 and Book Sends for $40, and I sold twenty-one units. So overall, I spent $128, sold forty-three books and received less than $15 in royalties. It was a terrible result.

Then I ran the free book promotion, and I uploaded my book to Freebooksy for $65. The result was that the book got downloaded 1,127 times within twenty-four hours. I did everything according to the plan, and transitioned the book from free to paid at a perfect moment, when the book was at the top of its rankings (115th place), but the following day I sold just two books…

As you can see, my experience with book promotion sites wasn't positive. I might try using their services for experimental purposes in the future, but overall, I think that there are much better ways to promote your books—for example, using Amazon Ads.

Use Amazon Ads to Sell More Books

When I launched my first book, I didn't even consider running ads. I thought I would just leave it on Amazon for organic sales. However, after a year or two, I was curious to try Amazon Ads to see how it works and what impact it may have on book sales. When I saw the result of Amazon Ads, I kept using them and I suggest you do that as well.

Below is the screenshot of the advertising metrics of my two books. It shows how much I've spent on advertising, how much was generated in book sales, and what the advertising cost of sales (ACOS) is. The ACOS is the percentage of attributed sales spent on advertising within fourteen days of clicks on your ads. This is calculated by dividing the total spend by attributed sales. As you can see, I spent $382.81 and generated $2,576.61 in book sales

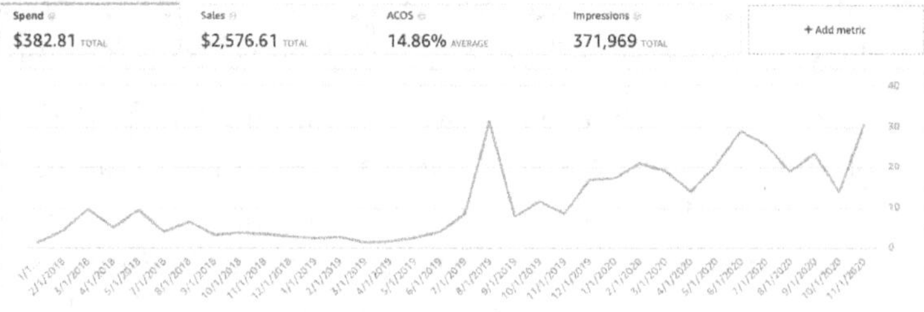

It's worth mentioning that the estimated sales and ACOS do not include Kindle Unlimited page reads (if your book is enrolled in KU), or audiobook sales (if you have it published). Sales on the Amazon Advertising (AMS) dashboard are based on the retail price of your book, not your royalties, so you need to calculate your actual return on investment (ROI) separately. If you know your royalty rate, it is not hard to calculate your ROI. For example:

- If your ebook is priced between $2.99–$9.99 and your royalty rate is 70%, then your ACOS should be less than 70% to get a positive ROI.

- If your ebook is priced below $2.99 or above $9.99 and your royalty rate is 35%, then your ACOS should be less than 35% to get a positive ROI.

- You get 60% (minus printing costs) royalties for paperback, which is around 40% of the retail price, so your ACOS should be less than 40% to get a positive ROI.

My average ACOS is 13.98%, which means I get a positive ROI. The ACOS can go up and down, so it's important to keep track of it and adjust your ads regularly. I run only "Sponsored Products" ads and haven't tried other options yet. In the beginning, I used a huge list of relevant keywords, but over time, I removed those that were not profitable. Now, running ads doesn't take much of my time; I review ad reports once per month, and if needed, I implement small changes—for example, removing unprofitable keywords or changing the bid price.

Setting up your campaign is pretty straightforward. Select the book you want to advertise, name your campaign, and set your budget. Different from Facebook Ads which will use all your budget, Amazon Ads will not use your budget if there are not enough people who click on your ads after typing the relevant keyword. Even though my daily budget is $20, I spend just $20–$30 on Amazon Ads each month because my keywords are quite specific. However, if your book has a broad audience, you may limit your budget to $5 at the beginning.

I recommend running "Sponsored Product" ads because they work for me and I hope they will work for you too. When you determine your targeting, you can let Amazon choose where to display your ad (Automatic targeting) or you may enter keywords yourself (Manual targeting). Even though creating a list of keywords takes time, I recommend doing so because this way, you can have more control. You can easily identify keywords by analyzing competing books. If you don't have time for that, choose "Automatic targeting"—Amazon algorithms work pretty well at determining what's the most relevant for its users.

Next, you need to set your bid—the maximum amount you are ready to pay for a click. When you do this for the first time, you can simply select the bid from a range that Amazon suggests. I recommend selecting the upper part of that range, or else your ad might not show up. You can adapt your bid later, based on your results. Finally, you should keep an eye on your ads' performance regularly. I recommend doing that one per month. If you see that some keywords are not profitable, you can pause them or reduce their bid.

Advertising on BookBub

BookBub is one of the best sites to promote your book, that's why I decided to review it separately. It has over ten million members who seek out new discounted books in genres that interest them, and offers book marketing tools to help authors sell more books. Compared with previously listed book promotion sites, BookBub is the most expensive, but its audience is more targeted and qualified, which means that you can expect a better return on your investment.

However, getting a BookBub promotion is not guaranteed. BookBub is highly selective of the books they feature in their newsletters, and their team of editors picks each day's Featured Deals from hundreds of submissions, ensuring they only feature great deals on quality ebooks. The platform accepts about 10–15% of the ebooks submitted for deals in the US. I have tried to apply to BookBub's Feature Deal, but I haven't been accepted.

If you want to try it too, first, you'll have to create a free BookBub Partner account, and claim your author profile. Only then you can apply for a Featured Deal or a Featured New Release through your author dashboard. BookBub displays their Featured Deals pricing and statistics here: https://www. bookbub.com/partners/pricing. The cost of a Featured Deal depends on the price of your book, the category you submit your book in, and which region you choose (United States or International). Here's an example of the category "General Nonfiction," which has over two million subscribers:

- If your book is free, you'll have to pay $421.

- If your book costs less than $1, you'll have to pay $612.

- If your book costs $1–$2, you'll have to pay $1,060.

- If your book costs $2–$3, you'll have to pay $1,531.

- If your book costs more than $3, you'll have to pay $2,143.

As you can see, the more your book costs, the more you'll pay for your book to be featured. Will it pay back? That's not guaranteed, but BookBub is very transparent with their statistics, and they share the average result that you can expect. If we suppose that your category is "General Nonfiction," and your book is free, you can expect on average 17,000 downloads, and if your book is paid, you can expect 1,710 sales. Let's take two examples:

- Your book costs $2.99 (you get 70% royalties) and the Featured Deal costs $1,531. If you sell 1,710 books, you would get $2.99*0.7*1,710=$3,579.03. Your ROI is positive—233.77%.

- Your book costs $0.99 (you get 35% royalties) and the Featured Deal costs $612. If you sell 1,710 books, you would get $0.99*0.35*1,710=$592.52. You experience $19.48 loss, but there's a chance that due to the boosted ranking you will sell more books on Amazon organically.

I encourage you to try BookBub, because it doesn't cost you anything to submit your book for a Featured Deal. You will have to pay only if your title is accepted. There are many authors who recommend this platform, and who get great results after being selected as the Featured Deal. If your title wasn't selected, you can re-submit your book after thirty days. I will certainly try to re-submit my books again in the future.

Find Your Own Methods That Help You Sell More Books

You can earn a badge on Amazon only if you *sell enough*. You can expect that Amazon will push your book only if you *sell enough on your own*. The entire Amazon algorithm operates on the principle that the platform will promote your book if you show that it sells.

If your book doesn't sell, why should Amazon promote it? It's not worth investing in something that is unproven. That is why you need to go the extra mile and bring some quality traffic to your book page. I have already mentioned that you should enroll your book in KDP Select, which has two promotional programs: Free Book Promotion and the Kindle Countdown Deal. However, to get the most of these programs, you must combine them with external marketing efforts, such as your own newsletter or book promotion sites. If you are just starting out, be prepared to invest money till you find what works best for you.

After interviewing crowdfunding creators, I learned that each of them found their own way to success. Using your personal and business contacts, reaching out to journalists and niche bloggers, influencer marketing, building a mailing list, writing a blog, running a podcast, posting relevant content on social media, advertising on Facebook/Google/Amazon. There are many marketing methods, and some of these methods may work for others, but may not work for you.

When I launched my first Kickstarter campaign, using my business network and keeping in touch with them by email, LinkedIn, and Skype helped me to get funded. Before releasing my second book, I didn't have an audience for which my book would be relevant, so I decided to go straight to Amazon. I found that Amazon Ads is a great method to get more sales without spending too much time on it. To find what works for me, I had to experiment and spend money on those things that didn't work. As you can see, I have shared different experiences—not only where I made money, but also where I lost. Hopefully this will help you to find your own way.

What Other Book Distribution Channels Should You Use?

There's a reason why the biggest part of this book covers the Kickstarter and Amazon platforms. Those two platforms brought the highest income for me personally. However, I keep experimenting with other distribution channels and want to share my findings with you.

As you have learned, I suggest launching a Kickstarter campaign for your book if you have at least 1,000–2,000 potential backers. Crowdfunding allows you to verify whether your book will meet a demand in the market and if so, you will get a chance to attract the first readers and increase the visibility of your book. After that, you should upload your book to Amazon, which is a great platform for growing your audience and selling more books.

When you upload your paperback to KDP, you can choose not only the various Amazon marketplaces, but also Expanded Distribution. This allows your book to be made broadly available outside of Amazon, and you can reach more readers through bookstores, online retailers, libraries, and academic institutions. The royalty rate for Expanded Distribution is 40% of the book's list price in the distribution channel, minus printing costs, applicable taxes, and withholding. An alternative option to Expanded Distribution is uploading your book to IngramSpark. If you sign up with IngramSpark, you won't be able to use the Expanded Distribution on KDP. So choose one option. If you choose KDP, it's easier to manage, and if you use IngramSpark, you will get higher royalties and will not depend on one platform.

Being dependent on one platform can be risky. My Amazon account was once temporarily suspended, and I don't know the exact reason for this even now. But feeling desperate and seeing that my hard work of a few years had suddenly disappeared encouraged me to think about how I could diversify my sales channels. That's the reason I use IngramSpark as an additional channel to sell my paperbacks (and I recommend you do so too), and I keep experimenting with other ebook stores and distribution channels.

Remember that if you enroll in KDP Select, your ebook must be sold exclusively on the Kindle Store for ninety days. Only after that can you upload your book to other distribution channels. I have tried Smashwords and Kobo, but the sales were very poor. Later, I uploaded my ebooks to IngramSpark and Draft2Digital. On IngramSpark, I had to choose all-or-nothing, and on Draft2Digital I could choose specific ebook stores. I simply selected those channels on Draft2Digital that were not available on IngramSpark. In addition to this, I uploaded my book directly to Apple. So far the results from all other ebook distribution channels aside KDP are poor, but I also didn't do any specific marketing.

Transforming Your Content into Other Formats

Writing a nonfiction book is a form of sharing your knowledge and expertise. However, you should not limit yourself to one format only. You can easily transform your content to other formats. If you've written a book, you should also consider publishing an audiobook or creating a video course.

Launching an audiobook is totally worth it if you've already published a book on Amazon. It doesn't cost that much to hire a professional narrator—for example, I paid $430 to have my book *Your First Kickstarter Campaign* narrated, which contained 55,000 words. The publishing process is very fast and the money you invest will pay you back very soon, as there are many people listening to audiobooks these days. Once you get your investment back, you can enjoy passive income from your audiobook.

The best way to publish your audiobook is by using the Audiobook Creation Exchange (ACX). It is a marketplace where you can find a professional narrator who will turn your book into an audiobook, and later it will be published on Audible, an online audiobook and podcast platform owned by Amazon. Unfortunately, ACX is not available for everyone. ACX is currently open to residents of the United States, United Kingdom, Canada, and Ireland who have a mailing address, valid local Taxpayer Identification Number (TIN), and banking details for one of these countries. If you are a resident of these countries, you should definitely open an account on ACX. If your country isn't supported by ACX, you can open an account on Findaway Voices, which can distribute your book to Audible (ACX) and other online audiobook platforms.

Another great way of transforming your content is creating an online video course. Whereas creating an audiobook is relatively easy—you just hire the right narrator and wait till he/she finishes the narration—building an online course is hard work…at least it was for me. First, you need to get high-quality video and audio equipment. You can film yourself with an iPhone—these days the video recording on smartphones is good enough—but for audio recording, it's better to use a separate microphone, such as Blue Yeti. Second, you need to create the right environment to record your course. It should be clean and your audio should sound good. Third, you will have to make adjustments to your content because a video course has a different structure to a book and should include some assignments. Finally, you will have to learn new skills: speaking in front of the camera, working with video editing programs, and uploading your course to the e-learning platform.

It took me seven months to create my first video course, based on my book. It wasn't easy, but it was truly an interesting experience, and I certainly recommend it to you. At least try and see if you feel comfortable doing this. When my course was finished, I uploaded it to Udemy, which is one of the largest global online learning and teaching marketplaces. I recommend Udemy only if you are a beginner because this platform has huge traffic and if your course ranks well, you can expect organic sales there. However, Udemy sells all courses at highly discounted prices, and students can get most courses for as low as $9.99, so there's not much left for the instructor. So if you have your own audience that is constantly growing, I would rather recommend using Teachable, Thinkific, Podia, Kajabi, or another similar platform that allows you to have full control of your course price.

Publishing an audiobook and creating a video course is just food for thought, and we won't discuss this topic here. Take it slowly, and begin your journey by turning your knowledge and expertise into a book. Once you've done that, you can start thinking about other ways of transforming your content, so you can reach new audiences.

IT'S YOUR TURN

"There is only one proof of ability – action."
—*Marie von Ebner-Eschenbach*

At this moment there are more than 15,000 successful publishing projects on Kickstarter. The majority of them received from $1,000 to $10,000 in pledges. I think that's a perfect goal for first-time authors. Now you have a proven strategy that you can use to launch your first book on Kickstarter, so get your MVP ready, build a crowd of potential backers, and start this journey!

I can guarantee that the preparation and launching process will be very rewarding, and you will learn a lot during this time. You will establish better relations with your readers—and trust me, they will be more excited to support you through Kickstarter than if you were to ask them to purchase your book on Amazon. Unlike a simple purchase through an estore, crowdfunding adds positive emotions and creates a direct bond between creator and backer. If you feel that you need more guidance on launching a Kickstarter project, you can read my book *Your First Kickstarter Campaign* (it's available as an ebook, paperback, and audiobook) or enroll in my course on the same topic on Udemy.

Once you've kept your promises and fulfilled your Kickstarter rewards, you will be ready to make your book available in public. A good thing about a successful crowdfunding campaign is that your backers have already paid for your self-publishing work and then you can upload your book to Amazon for free and enjoy a truly passive income from book sales.

That's all for now and I wish you all the best in your self-publishing journey! If you have any questions, feel free to reach out to me by email vilius.stanislovaitis@gmail.com.

P.S. You already know that reviews are extremely important for all authors. I hope this book was useful for you and I really appreciate your honest review. You can leave it on Amazon, GoodReads or other platform where you purchased this book. I read every single review and it means a lot for me personally. Thank you!

DOWNLOAD FREE BONUS

NONFICTION WRITING TIPS

Just to say thanks for reading my book,

I would like to give you this Free Bonus! Enjoy!
Go to: https://bit.ly/PublishYourKnowledge

ACKNOWLEDGMENTS

Enormous thanks to my beta readers who have reviewed the manuscript of this book and suggested what could be improved. Special thanks should be given to the following people:

- Angie Ferguson, who made a ton of comments. Angie has corrected thousands of research papers and books for years, so I received great benefit from Angie's suggestions.

- Caroline Keeber, who was the fastest to review the book. Just thanks to Caroline, I have corrected the part where I talk about MVP, so that it will be clearer for the readers. I hope I've managed to achieve this goal!

- Daiva Paskauskaite, who has not only reviewed the manuscript, but also suggested changes in the book structure and encouraged me to think more about my target reader.

- Danielius Goriunovas, who raised a few great questions that encouraged me to write additional content to make the book more informative and useful for the readers.

- Emiliya Karaboeva, who wrote extensive and extremely useful notes. Because of her comments, I decided to narrow my readership by emphasizing that this book is specialized for those who want to write nonfiction.

- Gedas Kucinskas, who is a man of few words. He reviewed my book from a marketing perspective and thanks to his suggestions, I decided to change the title of this book.

- Julia Good, who is an editor by profession and has done a "light proofread" with useful edits and great comments.

- Katherine Sgarbossa, who is a very warm and friendly person. She not only added useful comments on what to improve, but also said a few lovely compliments that made my day!

- Michael D. Young, who was very straight with his comments and constructive criticism. The more specific someone is when giving the feedback, the more actionable it is for me.

- Sergejs Petrovs, who has followed my writing journey from the first book. Sergejs helped me notice a few errors and provided great input on how to improve this book.

- Mike Cossaboom, who promised to be the first one to buy this book as soon as it is launched!

- Luke Ives Pontifell, the president of Thornwillow Press, which has launched thirty-one publishing projects on Kickstarter! I reached out to Luke by email and he instantly agreed to help me by sharing his crowdfunding experience.

Finally, I wish to thank my family and friends for their support and encouragement throughout my journey with this book.

www.ingramcontent.com/pod-product-compliance
Lightning Source LLC
LaVergne TN
LVHW010526200726

843506LV00013B/2713